Why You Should
Be a Trade Unionist

Why You Should Be a Trade Unionist

LEN McCLUSKEY

VERSO
London • New York

First published by Verso 2020
© Len McCluskey 2020

1 3 5 7 9 10 8 6 4 2

Verso
UK: 6 Meard Street, London W1F 0EG
US: 20 Jay Street, Suite 1010, Brooklyn, NY 11201
versobooks.com

Verso is the imprint of New Left Books

ISBN-13: 978-1-78873-787-6
ISBN-13: 978-1-78873-788-3 (UK EBK)
ISBN-13: 978-1-78873-789-0 (US EBK)

British Library Cataloguing in Publication Data
A catalogue record for this book is available from the British Library

Library of Congress Cataloging-in-Publication Data
A catalog record for this book is available from the Library of Congress
LCCN: 2019952254

Typeset in Monotype Fournier by Hewer Text UK Ltd, Edinburgh
Printed and bound by CPI Group (UK) Ltd, Croydon CR0 4YY

CONTENTS

ACKNOWLEDGEMENTS

A number of people have helped me with the writing of this book, but I would primarily like to thank Jennie Walsh, who worked closely with me for nearly two years, and without whom it would not have been possible. Any errors in the history I tell here are, however, entirely mine, as are the views I express.

Thanks to Howard Beckett, Charlotte Bence, Louisa Bull, Tony Burke, Gail Cartmail, Pauline Doyle, Victoria Egerton, Alex Flynn, Diana Holland, Sharon Graham, Liane Groves, Asif Mohammed, Jim Mowatt, Andrew Murray, Frances O'Grady, Mick Rix, Lauren Townsend, Steve Turner, Tony Woodhouse, John Usher and everyone else who helped me to focus my thoughts, recall memories, check facts and express why I believe we all should be trade unionists. My apologies to those colleagues and comrades who, over the decades of my own trade union activism, have been influential in shaping my politics, but whom I have not named. No one is forgotten.

Leo Hollis at Verso gave invaluable feedback and support in helping to shape the structure and direction of the book, as did Andrew Murray. Thanks, too, to Mark Martin and Tim Clark at Verso for their skilful copy editing. It was a remarkably pain-free experience.

This book has been researched and written during extraordinary and polarised times in British politics. As it goes to press, we are in full general election campaign mode. I sincerely hope that by the time *Why You Should Be a Trade Unionist* reaches bookshops that this nation has achieved a lasting, credible settlement, one that heals our divisions and gives hope of a fairer future for all the people of this country.

Len McCluskey
November 2019

1

HOPE IN MY HEART

Just look him in his eyes and say
We're gonna do it anyway
                                    Labi Siffre

I joined the Transport and General Workers' Union
(T&G) more than fifty years ago, when at the age of eighteen I started work as a plan man on the Liverpool docks. As
I walked through the dock gates on my first day, someone
gave me a form and said: 'You join the union here, son.'

At the time, I had a choice of jobs and the expectation
of job security. In fact, I was only intending to work on the
docks for a year. I had been accepted at a teaching college in
Birmingham. My mate, John Foley, who was coming with
me to college, decided to take a year off (long before gap
years had been invented), and I did not want to go without him. He went on to become a brilliant head teacher,

for forty years. I got a job and waited for him. I actually got three job offers and only made up my mind which one to take the day before I was due to start. The other jobs were in insurance, a much safer bet in those days. But I chose the path less trodden and started work for the Port of Liverpool Stevedoring Company.

Liverpool was a trade union city and I knew what unions were. I came from a working-class family, living in a two-up-two-down house, with parents who used to say they'd cut their arms off before they'd ever vote Tory. I didn't have to fight for my right to join a union – others had done that before me – and I was soon actively involved in mine.

I was a child of the 1960s. Revolution was in the air: in dress, music and politics, and, of course, with the civil rights movement in America, Northern Ireland and Vietnam. The docks were a brilliant and vibrant place to be a young man; they were filled with the most knowledgeable and funny people who taught me a lot. Not all of them were sympathetic to the long-haired, left-wing students protesting in Paris and the United States, but the Liverpool dockers understood class issues. These included what was happening in Chile and South Africa, and our debates were informed by the feeling that an attack on one trade unionist was an attack on all of us.

Not long after getting involved in the union, and winning a fight for younger workers to be paid the same as their older colleagues, I was persuaded to become a shop steward, a position I held for the next ten years, quickly reaching senior shop steward. People then started suggesting I should become a union officer. I didn't really know what this involved, other than it meant working full-time for the union and would take me away from my beloved Liverpool docks after eleven very happy years working there. But I hoped I might be good at it, so in 1979 I applied, and a fortnight later I was appointed a T&G regional officer. I was based in Merseyside, but my remit increasingly spread throughout the North West.

As a regional officer I was involved with just about every sector in which the T&G represented workers. I was active in every trade group, from transport to auto manufacturing to agriculture and the voluntary sector. After ten years I had risen to the position of national secretary, and then in 2004 I was named assistant general secretary. Finally, seven years later, I was appointed general secretary of Unite the Union, which had been formed in 2007 as a result of a merger between the T&G and Amicus.

This was a period of tremendous upheaval. Some of the responsibility for that turbulence has to go to a person who got a promotion the same year I became a regional officer. In 1979 Margaret Thatcher was elected as prime minister, famously declaring that there is 'no such thing as society'. Or rather: 'I'm all right, Jack.' The idea that the only reason any of us are on this earth is just to look after ourselves was, to me, a repellent creed, alien to how I was brought up and to the world I wanted to see flourish. As I started my work across Merseyside and the North West, I saw a region, and a community, increasingly devastated by Thatcher's vindictive policies towards ordinary working people, their industries and their unions.

I was very much in the middle of that storm. This was during the so-called Militant years of Liverpool City Council, and I was deeply involved in the Broad Left of my union at both regional and national levels. I was passionate about developing resistance to the onslaught of Thatcherism. For me, that kind of political work, alongside our industrial work, was fundamental to why we should be trade unionists. And today, having been a union general secretary through the long years of Tory austerity, I've become ever more convinced that the trade union movement offers the only pathway to ensuring a better, more united future.

Without doubt, my experiences in my first job on the docks were far removed from the realities of the world of work faced by young people today. The industrial landscape has been changed fundamentally by the decimation of our great manufacturing industries. It is over ten years since the bankers broke the economy, and now we have an emerging workforce that has only known austerity. Furthermore, over the last three decades, government policy has created a world hostile to trade unions and a society that treats working people with a distinct lack of dignity and respect. Today, more than 80 per cent of our economy is in the service sector, bringing with it insecure, low-paid employment and precarious zero-hour contracts. With impunity, bosses feel empowered to tell workers, illegally, that they have no right to join a trade union, or threaten that they will be sacked if they do so.

Not long before I started work on the Liverpool docks, dockers used to gather at the beginning of the working day in what were called pens, such was the casualised nature of dock labour then. The comparison to cattle pens was apt, as they were treated like animals. The workers were hoping for a day or a half-day's work, just to put food on the table. Often they had to fight each other to get hold of the brass tally – which they needed in order to work – thrown down on the floor by the bosses. My union won its victory against this casualisation in 1967, when the Devlin Report heralded the outlawing of such demeaning practices and the decasualisation of dock labour, making a permanent difference to the dockers' and their families' lives.

Victories like this, won by the unions, should be a lesson to all of us as we face the challenges of overturning the new, unregulated, casualised labour practices that are so pervasive today. It is absolutely shameful that the rights of the worker continue to be so ruthlessly undermined. This is precisely why trade unions were so important back then, and why they are more necessary today than they ever have been. It is crucial then, in making the case for being a trade unionist to those who may never have encountered or considered joining one, to explain just what a trade union is and does.

In 2018, trade union membership stood at 6.3 million, an increase of 100,000 on the previous year and more than in any year since the turn of the century. There are now forty-eight trade unions in the UK affiliated to the Trades Union Congress (TUC), representing workers across all sectors of the economy, from manufacturing to banking, agriculture to midwifery, hospitality to social media, and the NHS to professional football. We are a long way from our peak membership of 13 million in 1979, and the causes of that decline are also an important story to tell.

A trade union is an organisation made up of members who are workers. It brings people together to make their lives better: to win better pay, to ensure safer and more inclusive workplaces, and to improve access to skills and training. Trade unionists look out for each other, and when a group of workers act and speak together, their employer has to listen.

Anyone who has a job, or even anyone looking for one, should be in a union. Unions negotiate with employers on pay and conditions. They fight to protect the workforce when major changes, such as large-scale job losses, are proposed. They represent individual members at disciplinary and grievance hearings. Unions also provide members with legal and financial advice, and a wide range of other benefits. For example, National Union of

Journalists (NUJ) members can get into museums and galleries around the world for free using the NUJ press card. On average, union members receive higher pay than non-members. They are also likely to get better sickness and pension benefits, more paid holiday, and more control over things like shifts and working hours.

Trade unionism has a long and deep history. In 1834 a group of agricultural workers in the Dorset village of Tolpuddle – James Brine, James Hammett, George Loveless, James Loveless, John Standfield and Thomas Standfield – formed the Friendly Society of Agricultural Labourers in response to decreasing wages. Collectively, they demanded ten shillings a week. They were punished for their activities and charged with taking an illegal oath. All six men were transported to the penal colonies. But their real 'crime', in the eyes of the ruling class, and in particular for their landed employers, was their attempt to form a trade union. In response, over 800,000 people signed a petition demanding the release of the abused heroes. The Tolpuddle Martyrs were among the pioneers of the early trade union and workers' rights movements, and we celebrate them each year with a festival in their Dorset village.

Such bravery resonates still. In more recent times, another group of workers said loud and clear that enough was enough and joined together to campaign for their rights. Sick of having their card tips taken by their employer, front-of-house staff at the high street restaurant chain TGI Fridays decided they would form a trade union in order to defend their rights at work. They were soon joined by staff at the pub chain Wetherspoons and by McDonald's workers demanding an end to zero-hour contracts, low pay and youth rates. Together they recruited, organised, mobilised – and walked out. They became trade unionists in order to win their collective rights. And while they didn't achieve all their demands, they won significant improvements.

To some, such collective action might appear to be rather out of date. The decline in trade union membership – which has taken place in parallel with deliberate deindustrialisation policies, anti-union laws and the changing nature of work – has to an extent created a vicious circle in which unions are portrayed in the mainstream media as irrelevant. At the same time, workers, and particularly young workers, have been given the impression that unions do not or, worse, cannot represent them. The precarious nature of much of today's work often makes it difficult for those in insecure, zero-hour jobs to see what unions might do for them.

When the BBC journalist Nick Robinson put it to me during his *Political Thinking* podcast that gig economy jobs are great because they're 'no hassle, no bother, an easy way [for people] to top up their wages, especially for students and the recently retired', my reaction was one of anger.[1] Robinson's implication was that such jobs are a convenient option because they offer flexible work. What he refused to acknowledge was that most of the millions of people working in insecure jobs and on zero-hour contracts have little choice but to be subjected to such precarious flexibility. Most workers want proper wages and an employment contract that gives them rights. Which is why they need trade unions.

The TGI Fridays dispute undoubtedly countered Robinson's argument. The workers' achievements gave the lie to the assumption that there is no point in joining a trade union if you're young, working in the precarious gig economy, and if your employer doesn't recognise a union.

This campaign also reminded us that unions need to adapt to remain relevant in giving working people the courage to fight injustice. Every time a journalist challenges me on the relevance of unions to today's so-called gig economy, I agree: unions have to be relevant to each and every sector, and not just to try to recruit in them, but actually organise and win victories for the workers. Through its campaigning, organising and political, community and educational work, the trade union movement must continually adapt and modernise in order to make itself relevant to today's world of work.

My trade union hero, Jack Jones, made such an impact on me when, as a young shop steward on the docks, I read his pamphlet 'A World to Win'.[2] In it he evoked a world where bigotry, injustice and oppression had been eliminated for the common good. It stirred a fire in me, a flame of hope and determination to achieve a better, fairer society, a flame which still burns brightly. Working people today need that hope as much as they ever did.

Consider what a world without unions would be like, whether in the past, the present or the uncertain future. This is perhaps the most powerful argument there is for being a trade unionist. In writing this short book, I've set out to demonstrate why people today should be trade union members. It is told through my personal experiences, as well as through a study of the history of trade unions and of the work they have done, and are doing, to make our workplaces and society fairer. This is work that is rarely portrayed positively by the press, if at all. The history of trade unions – of when and why they emerged in the UK as democratic organisations giving a voice to working people, and of why opposition to them developed – is fundamental to making the case for trade unionism today.

But trade unionism is not just about pay and conditions. It's about diversity, putting equality at work and in society front and centre stage; it's about community, politics, internationalism and much more. I believe strongly in rebuilding the traditional, if at present weakened, links between trade unions and communities. Being a trade unionist is as much a political as it is an industrial role. This is why the historic links between the labour movement and the Labour Party matter.

This book is intended as a bold reminder of how trade

unions have achieved justice through their collective, united strength. It is also a call to arms for the struggles that lie ahead.

2

GIVING A VOICE

The labour movement was the principal force that transformed misery and despair into hope and progress.

Martin Luther King Jr

In a time when our children learn little more history than Kings and Queens in school, the working class must tell its own story. In August 2019 we marked the 200th anniversary of the Peterloo Massacre, the moment when our journey to working-class representation and respect began, when working-class people stood up for democracy and economic political freedom, and were brutally crushed for their proud defiance. Eighteen peaceful protestors were killed by the cavalry troops who swept into St Peter's Field with their sabres drawn. Some were trampled by the stampede, others were shot by muskets fired indiscriminately into the crowd.

Mike Leigh, the film director who made the 2018 film *Peterloo*, tells of how he went to school within 'spitting distance' of St Peter's Field in Manchester. Yet even he and his school mates didn't learn about the atrocity. Today, as they did then, the ruling class would prefer to sweep Peterloo, and all other such brutal injustices against working people, under the table. This is precisely why we must teach our own history and fight for our own justice.

What that history tells us is that progress for working people has only ever been achieved by the collective self-empowerment of organised labour, not through the accumulation of individual rights alone, however worthy they may be.

Employers have always been effective at working together to control labour. As far back as medieval times, the masters organised themselves into guilds to regulate prices, quality standards and their workers' wages, even imposing sanctions on workers for coming up short. There was no voice then for those they employed. Then as now, workers were legislated against in order to keep them down. At the beginning of the nineteenth century, the Combination Acts, passed during the Napoleonic wars, made any sort of strike action illegal. Workers could be imprisoned for up to three months or sentenced to brutal hard labour if they broke the new laws.

Despite the Combination Acts, workers continued to press for better pay and working conditions, and trade unions grew rapidly. The Acts were finally repealed in

1824–5, but the repression of trade unions and trade unionists during the industrial revolution continued. This was
the fate of the Tolpuddle Martyrs in the 1830s, but they
were not alone.[1]

It was the Chartist movement of the 1840s that laid
down the foundations of our modern labour movement.
The Chartists coalesced around a People's Charter that set
out six electoral reforms aimed at extending the franchise
and enabling working men to be elected to Parliament. The
Chartists also did much to organise non-unionised workers, holding regular mass demonstrations and instructing
uneducated people in the basics of organising meetings
and campaigning.

Such protests steadily improved the conditions of working men and women. The 1847 Ten Hours Act restricted
the working hours of women and young workers in textile
mills, though this was not extended to adult men until 1850.
It was a long-fought-for victory that galvanised the unions
into further organisation, leading to the formation of the
Trades Union Congress in Manchester in 1868, the legali-
sation of unions through the 1871 Trade Union Act, and
the start of campaigns for the eight-hour day, the repeal of
anti-union laws, extension of the franchise, and the unioni-
sation of the railways. It also led to the establishment of
many new unions, including the National Amalgamated
Stevedores and Dockers Union (the first dock workers'
union in the UK) and the Miners' Federation of Great
Britain, as well as the emergence of unions within Jewish

immigrant communities working in the baking and clothing trades.

There were early interventions by women trade unionists too. In 1872 a National Union of Agricultural Workers was set up in Warwickshire. The following year a group of sixteen women from Ascott-under-Wychwood demanded that their association be represented. They were imprisoned in 1873 for picketing in support of male agricultural workers, and were only pardoned following an appeal to Queen Victoria. Only recently have these brave women workers, the Ascott Martyrs, begun to be honoured in our collective trade union memories.

The history of our movement is also the history of the struggle by the left to secure for working people the unions and the leaders they need and deserve. In the 1880s, what became known as 'new unionism' emerged in reaction to the perceived ineffectiveness of the TUC, which was hostile to a model of industrial unionism in which all workers in an industry are organised into the same union, regardless of their skills. New unionism was undoubtedly a turning point that saw trade unions reaching out beyond the skilled and craft elite of the working class.

The London 'match girls' strike of 1888 was a key moment in new unionism, involving working-class women and teenage girls, uneducated and starving, slogging long hours for Bryant and May on slave wages, physically and mentally abused by their bosses, and exposed to lethal white phosphorus that rotted their jaw bones and led to horrific deaths.[2] They became determined fighters and trade unionists, and by walking out on strike and closing the factory for sixteen days, they secured improvements in their working conditions, including recognition of their union.

Tom Mann was a key figure in the new unionism movement, and one of the chief organisers of the 1889 London dockers' strike for union recognition, the abolition of contract work, and a minimum wage of sixpence an hour (the 'dockers' tanner').[3] For me, the dockers' strike and the Taff Vale Railway strike of 1900 were among the key moments in our history that gave the unions greater confidence to organise and fight.[4] The dock strike involved thousands, and, as Terry McCarthy says in his short history of the British Labour movement, the strike leaders won over the public with their shrewd tactics.[5] There were no slogans about overthrowing the state, and no violent protests; instead, the trade unions took the people with them, and won. Furthermore, for the first time, the new unionism focused on workplace issues beyond hours and conditions, including the huge deductions imposed on women clothing workers for things like the use of cooking facilities and, extraordinarily, the use of steam power, even if they were working from home.

The Taff Vale strike also ultimately convinced the trade unions of the need for a Labour Party to give workers a voice in Parliament. In the South Wales valleys, determined members of the Amalgamated Society of Railway

Servants (ASRS), a forerunner to today's RMT, resisted their employers and unjust laws. Nevertheless, the bosses took the ASRS to court for lost earnings and won a staggering £42,000 in damages – the equivalent of well over £2 million today. It was this travesty, decided in the House of Lords, that persuaded the unions they needed representation in the House of Commons in order to pass legislation that would improve workers' lives, rather than just challenge existing laws from the outside.

The results of this change in tactics were seen in the Trade Disputes Act of 1906, which reversed the whittling away of union rights granted by the 1871 Trade Union Act. The 1906 Act legalised peaceful picketing, and prevented employers from taking legal action against workers for 'breach of contract' if it was done in pursuit of a trade dispute. Back then, this had a far wider definition than it does now, including enabling workers to withdraw their labour in support of others not employed by the same employer. The Act also protected trade union funds, but the biggest victory was the clause that exempted trade unions from legal action. These were rights and protections all reversed by Thatcher's laws.

This was the start of working people's challenge to Toryism, with its class hierarchy and its determination to always put private property before freedom and democracy. It was also a challenge to liberalism, which will do anything for the poor so long as the poor never organise to do anything for themselves. Indeed, in the late nineteenth century, it was the refusal by the then Liberal Party to speak up for an increasingly organised working class that not only helped to drive the formation of trade unions, but also led to the foundation of the Labour Party.

By the early twentieth century, trade unions were becoming central to society, in spite of the hostility they faced. They began to be portrayed in popular culture, most notably with the 1914 publication of Robert Tressell's *The Ragged Trousered Philanthropists*, one of the greatest books of all time. Anyone wanting to understand the world of work should read it. It is shameful that, in today's zero-hour wastelands, and with so many people struggling to live on the minimum wage, nothing has changed since Tressell's story of the efforts by the painter and decorator, Frank Owen, to make ends meet and convince his colleagues that capitalism was the cause of their troubles. Tressell's depiction of the 'great money trick' is so simple, and yet millions of workers have been captured by it ever since.

The First World War was an opportunity for the unions to organise and to politicise workplaces, and there was a significant increase in union membership, not least among the women who kept the factories going while the men fought abroad. Nevertheless, at the same time there was a more concerted effort by the state to undermine the Labour Party, left-wing unions and their leaders, not by brute force but through an ideological campaign of vilification and smears, aided eagerly by the Tory press.

Unfortunately, the history of trade unions is littered with examples of rank-and-file trade unionists being let down by their leaders. In 1925, the agreement by the government to avert strikes by negotiating a subsidy for the coal industry to enable the employers to maintain wages and conditions was a short-lived victory. Soon the employers were again demanding wage cuts and a longer working week, and when the miners launched industrial action in 1926 under the slogan 'not a penny off the pay or an hour on the day', many workers walked out in solidarity. Although the TUC called a general strike, a combination of weak leadership and government determination to support the employers led to the strike's defeat.

The Second World War underpinned the strength of trade unionism, which was significantly invigorated as the country prepared for conflict with the building of ships and the manufacture of munitions. Employment increased across the country, including among women, who were again called up to work in the factories and became increasingly active in the labour movement. This new confidence led to the growth of the shop stewards' movement that organised the union rank and file across the country. The period also saw a growth in white-collar trade unionism.

When Clement Attlee's Labour government came to power in 1945, repealing Tory anti-union laws, approving closed shops, nationalising key industries and establishing the NHS and the welfare state, the confidence and strength of the unions grew further. This was a government that worked hand in hand with the unions, and its major reforms were union-driven, including the extension of workers' rights and the establishment of the Agricultural Wages Board. Sick-pay schemes were introduced, and the Dock Labour Scheme of 1947 set a guaranteed minimum fallback wage and created job security for registered dockers. It was abolished by Thatcher in 1989.

By the time Harold Wilson's Labour government was elected in 1964, the then general secretary of T&G, Frank Cousins, was appointed minister of technology. This was the start of a new era of militancy, with Cousins leading the opposition to any dilution of the socialist principles of the Labour Party, and eventually resigning from the government in protest at its enforcement of an incomes policy that held back wages.

Jack Jones, Cousins' successor at the top of the T&G, went on to cement a formidable left-wing alliance with Hugh Scanlon, leader of the engineering union, and together they halted Labour's plans to place legal restrictions on industrial action and on the shop stewards' movement. These were formulated in *In Place of Strife*, a 1969 White Paper drawn up by Barbara Castle, the secretary of state for employment and productivity, which proposed an Industrial Board to enforce settlements in industrial disputes. The Jones–Scanlon partnership, with a mass movement behind them, effectively killed off the cabinet vote in favour of the plans.

The pair then played a central role in the development of a militant rank-and-file movement against the incoming Conservative government's anti-trade union laws. This was a movement that saw the London dockers challenge and defeat the government, mass solidarity with the miners, and a wave of over 200 workplace occupations that began to challenge the conventions of capitalist ownership.

I remember well the TUC march against the draconian 1971 Industrial Relations Act brought in by Ted Heath's Conservative government. The Act included powers to sequestrate union assets and to prevent mass picketing and secondary action. It also sought to limit strikes through the establishment of a National Industrial Relations Court (NIRC), empowered to grant injunctions against unions and to settle disputes – not unlike the *In Place of Strife* plan – as well as enable no-strike clauses in individual contracts.

To go to prison in the cause of trade union freedom is not something many trade unionists in Britain have had to face, but five brave dockers did just that. The Pentonville Five, as they became known, were arrested for refusing to appear before the NIRC and were imprisoned in the summer of 1972, after an unofficial strike at the Chobham Farm container depot in Newham, London. They were released after six days when the Official Solicitor applied to the Court of Appeal to have the arrest warrants overturned. The subsequent protests of working people against this direct attack on their trade union organisations eventually forced the government to step back from the Act.

Another group of workers imprisoned during this period of Tory war against the trade unions was the Shrewsbury 24, who were arrested in 1972 following the national building workers' strike to secure better wages and safety regimes. Two of them – Des Warren and the now household name (and my good friend) Ricky Tomlinson – were found guilty of conspiracy to intimidate for visiting building sites and trying to persuade non-union workers to down tools. Tomlinson's fight to clear his and Warren's names continues to this day.[6]

Next came victory for the miners' in 1974, when their strike in demand of better pay effectively brought down Heath's government. The prime minister's response to the government pay board's decision to recommend the NUM's pay claim was to call a snap general election in February, with the campaign slogan 'Who governs Britain?' The poll resulted in a hung Parliament, leading to another election in October in which Labour was returned to power with a very narrow majority.

During the following five-year term – with first Wilson, then Jim Callaghan as prime minister – there were significant gains for the unions in terms of health and safety legislation. These included the 1974 Health and Safety at Work Act and the 1977 Safety Representatives Regulations, with their vital statutory rights for trade union health and safety reps. By now the long march of the labour movement had achieved democracy and the welfare state, while living standards had taken great strides forward and the labour share of income was the highest it has ever been. It was also in this period that trade union membership reached its peak, with over 13 million members by 1979.

But it was also the time that leading members of the Tory hard-right – including Margaret Thatcher, Keith Joseph, Norman Tebbit and Nicholas Ridley – realised that if they ever got back into power they would have to curb trade union strength. Which they duly did, through the orchestration of salami-style legislation, year on year, throughout the 1980s. Act upon parliamentary Act restricted our ability to take lawful industrial action and picket workplaces, with secondary 'sympathy' action being outlawed. Employers were handed new and powerful legal means to stop strikes if unions put a foot wrong, including in how they balloted their members and the ballot thresholds they must reach. What counted as a trade dispute was now so narrowly defined so as to restrict what we could actually take action about.

Why did Thatcher and her successors do this? Because employers and the political establishment knew then, and understand even more acutely now, that trade unions are the first line of defence for working people. It amuses me whenever the right-wing media try to portray trade unions as being irrelevant – with membership today less than half what it was at the end of the 1970s – because I always think, if we're so irrelevant then why do they keep attacking us? Why don't they just leave us alone and let us wither on the vine? They don't, because they know that we are the only ones who challenge their power, the only ones able to stand up to them.

What does this brief history of British trade unionism demonstrate? Firstly, that the story is inextricably linked to working-class history, and that working-class people have consistently been given a voice by becoming trade unionists.

When I worked on the docks in Liverpool, I remember how an arch-Conservative friend of a family member challenged me about why I'd become a trade unionist and shop steward. It's a bit of a Monty Python cliché, but he said: 'What have the unions ever done for you?' I told him my union had given me a voice, and dignity at work. And I've never come up with a better answer since. My experience on the docks taught me so much about the essence of solidarity, being able to stand up with dignity, look an employer in the eye, and not be intimidated.

And that's exactly what our British Airways mixed fleet have done recently, reminding us that the struggles of the past continue to be the challenges of the present. During a lobby of Parliament, MPs were visibly shaken when BA mixed fleet cabin-crew members, on strike to secure an increase in the poverty pay the airline forced them to live on, told them about their working conditions and the creative methods BA was using to avoid paying them the minimum wage, including by lumping in food allowances.

Among those sharing their stories of living on pot noodles and tins of tuna, sleeping overnight in their cars, being unable to afford fuel to get to work, and losing incentive pay for being sick, there was a deep resolve not to be cowed by our national carrier. A deep resolve even though the airline was punishing them for their action by denying them their bonuses – those hard-earned extras that are vital to workers whose take home annual salary amounts to just over £12,000.

These mixed fleet members, the majority of them young, took some eighty-five days of industrial action, in what became one of the longest running disputes in recent trade union history. They weren't being greedy. They just wanted to be able to provide the best and safest service they could to BA customers, and to be paid a wage they could live on for doing so. Trade unionism gave them a voice to demand that they be treated with dignity.

I recall some of the conversations I had with those on strike – whose jobs are considered so glamorous by the public – when I joined them on the Heathrow picket line:

'I've had to have a second job the entire six years I've worked on mixed fleet. My BA pay covers my rent and no more.'

'There are some routes where we have no choice but to stay in the crew hotel and eat there, at huge expense.'

'It makes me rage when I see the profits BA is making, but none of it is passed on to its workers. All they need do is offer us a bit more money, give us our bonuses back and treat us with a bit of respect.'

The mixed fleet members were inspired to take their stand by BA cabin-crew colleagues before them, members of our British Airlines Stewards and Stewardesses Association (BASSA), who had been in dispute with the airline for nearly two years over staff cuts – a dispute I was heavily involved in settling in 2011.[7] This was a very high-profile and heroic struggle, and I was privileged to represent this group of decent people who stood firm and defeated BA's CEO Willy Walsh, the darling of the right-wing media. Similarly, it was the determination and solidarity of our mixed fleet members, and the voice trade unionism gave them, that secured a decent pay rise in the end. They stuck together through thick and thin, and demonstrated how it pays to be a trade unionist.

The vast majority of trade unionists' time is spent dealing positively with employers over pay and conditions and resolving grievances, and I am proud of the type of engagement we have with them. I talk to company chief executives every week, often working together to resolve complex issues that as an employer they cannot solve on their own. That is what unions and their shop stewards do – they negotiate and work to put out fires. We do not seek confrontation, and we do not relish fights; but neither do we walk away from bullying bosses and companies that are not treating their employees fairly. We are afraid of no one.

So when we do take industrial action, it is a last resort. And it is how workers find their voice when their employer is refusing to hear it.

Another example: Greenwich Leisure Ltd (GLL) runs libraries and swimming pools for local authorities in London, many of which have London Living Wage (LLW) accreditation, meaning they should mandate GLL to pay the LLW. But some have allowed the firm to pay eighteen- to twenty-year-olds over £2 an hour less. So we built a campaign, talking to those young workers about what mattered to them, bringing them into union membership, and putting political and industrial pressure on the local authorities, supposedly so proud of their LLW accreditation, through protests, lobbies of council meetings and media activity.

Finding a voice through their trade unionism, these young workers were able to force councillors to explain why they were letting a private contractor off the hook when it came to ensuring fair and equal pay. The decision of the Waltham Forest and Tower Hamlets councils to pay under-twenty-ones the LLW were big wins that saw a significant number of young Londoners joining Unite.

The list of similar campaigns is long. The TGI Fridays dispute, the Pizza Express fair tips campaign,[8] the McDonald's strike, and the fair pay deals we've struck for hospitality workers at the Edinburgh fringe,[9] have all been made possible because young people working in hospitality are standing up and taking action. They know why they should be trade unionists.

Asif Mohammed chairs Unite's West Midlands regional and young members' committees. He recorded a video in which he explains why he became a trade unionist:

> I joined Unite as a student, when I worked in retail. I saw there was a lot of exploitation, including non-payment of the adult national living wage rate. I thought the best way to challenge this was by becoming part of a collective, coming together with people who were in a similar position as me and fighting for better pay and conditions, and ultimately achieving a better, fairer future for all of us.

Asif had a piece of advice for young people starting out in work today. Joining a union will give them a voice both at work and within the union. His point is that members are central to the democratic life of any trade union, and there are many ways to be involved. Asif's rise to chair of a Unite regional committee, in his early twenties, also demonstrates the new vibrancy that our young members are bringing to our union. We are seeing young trade unionists, with women at the fore, generating an enthusiasm that is so necessary in any organisation, carrying forward the values of older members and expressing those values in different ways. And this is fantastic for the future of our movement.

3

UNITY IS STRENGTH

A trade union is like a bundle of sticks. A worker who is not in a union is like a single stick. She can easily be broken or bent to the will of her employer. An employer can do without one worker. He cannot do without all his workers.

Mary Macarthur (1880–1921)

Too often we hear the lament: 'I can't join a union because there isn't one where I work.' But all trade unions have to start somewhere, and it does not require the prior approval of union officials, or recognition by an employer, for a union to exist. The history of trade unions demonstrates that they are essentially no more than a group of workers coming together to defend rights that are under attack, to demand rights they do not yet have, and to improve pay and conditions.

The first thing a would-be activist needs to do is find the appropriate union to join. The TUC hosts a find-a-union service on its website.[1] Some unions, including Unite, have an online joining facility, so there is no need to make a phone call during working hours or to arrange a clandestine meeting with a union official in order to sign up. At the same time, the new union member will need to talk to colleagues about the issues they are unhappy or concerned about – long hours, fair pay, overtime, health and safety, bullying, sexual harassment, and so on – and persuade them that by joining together in a union they can address these issues and make demands. But there's no magic wand – the mere act of a few people joining a union won't solve such problems. Only by standing together collectively can we do that.

Let's assume we have a workplace of young people in, say, the IT or hospitality sectors, where union membership is low but dissatisfaction high, and exploitative working practices are widespread. The TGI Fridays activists, for example, built their union starting with only a handful of members; they were not going to wait for a union to approach them. They used WhatsApp, Facebook and other online platforms to persuade and support colleagues in restaurants around the country.

The result was a strike that emerged from below, one that did not need a union headquarters to run it. Instead, just a handful of members began to recruit and organise in their own way, building a union based on collectivism and the recognition of shared conditions. They swiftly realised that there is power in numbers and that their voice was stronger as a collective. This in turn gave them the confidence needed to win support for a strike ballot. The TGI workers chose to join Unite. Workers at McDonald's and Wetherspoons went for the bakers' union, the BFAWU. Others in precarious sectors, such as Uber, have gone with the GMB, and we're also seeing people in the gig economy joining what are being dubbed 'pop-up' unions like the IWGB (Independent Workers Union of Great Britain).

In another example, Google UK may have a fabulous new headquarters building in London's King's Cross, but the workplace issues that its staff encounter are as commonplace as in any other office. Sexual harassment and a lack of pay transparency are just the most obvious. There was no union at Google UK, but one employee was convinced they needed one and took the first step. They contacted our local rep and met for a chat in a pub. Leaflets were produced and before long there was a core membership of about thirty. It was not a lot, but it was a start, and it resulted in our members, and other Google employees in London, joining the international walkout in 2018 over how the company tackles allegations of sexual harassment.[2] On this occasion union membership gave workers the strength to stand up to unacceptable behaviour in the workplace. Is this why people are so scared of trade unions?

Rebecca Long-Bailey, the shadow industry secretary as I write, was once asked by a journalist whether Labour's policies on empowering trade unions, enabling them to work alongside a Labour government, were not something of a problem. Wouldn't people be afraid of unions 'taking over'? Rebecca asked him if he knew what a union was. I am not sure if he did, but she told him anyway: 'A union is a group of workers, it can be as big or as small as you like. But it's about those workers coming together collectively to demand respect at work, a safe working environment, decent pay,' she explained. 'Not only that, they are economically beneficial to employers.'

Unity is strength, on the factory floor, in the office, on the building site, in the restaurant, on the road – wherever we sell our labour.

Arriving at the Oxford Bus picket line in 2017, I was hit by a wall of sound.[3] Passing car drivers, many of whom would usually use the city's bus service, and HGV drivers at the neighbouring lorry depot, were sounding their horns in support of our members, who had walked out over a total breakdown in industrial relations. The support from local people was phenomenal. The strikers were fighting a deeply hostile employer who had refused to give their low-paid workers a pay rise. On that occasion, it gave me great pride to announce that our union would double the strike pay for our members so they could continue their fight for fair treatment.

Such an announcement sends an unequivocal message to an intransigent employer: the workers will not be starved back to work. As a consequence, when I crossed the road to visit him in his office, the Oxford Bus boss was quick to restore the ripped-up recognition agreement with Unite, and the dispute was won. Trade union strike funds ensure that our members in dispute do not lose their voice when their money runs out. The Tory press considers these funds to be a somehow sinister and bullying aspect of trade unionism, but they simply even up the fight.[4]

What was my role in this action? The political journalist Robert Peston once introduced me on his show as the 'last of the union barons', and warmed to his theme as the interview progressed. I did not challenge him at the time – there were bigger issues to debate – but it is a term that conjures up tired old images of behind-closed-doors, stitched-up deals between unions, governments and bosses.

I dare say that if I was the union baron Peston credited me as, I would cherry pick the disputes that the union supports. I would be cautious about putting Unite's resources behind actions against powerful, notoriously anti-union employers, whose aim is to break us, not talk to us. But here is the truth: members are central to the democratic life of trade unions, and it's not for me, or any other general secretary, to renounce or reject the struggles that members embark on.

Too often union leaders have found excuses for not supporting striking members, which often leads to sell-outs, and leaves a bitter aftertaste. My friends on the Liverpool docks can testify to that. For two-and-a-half years, from 1995 to 1998, they mounted a magnificent dispute after being sacked for refusing to cross the picket line of colleagues employed by a different company. It was one of the longest industrial disputes in British history, and the dockers were the epitome of what trade unionism is all about. Those brave workers never gave up hope.[5] However, the dispute was not my union's finest hour and they were ultimately sold out, never getting their jobs back, because the leadership refused to support them.

This underlines the importance of lay member control of unions, and Tony Woodhouse, who is the chair of Unite's executive council, is a principled example of this.

I am proud that I have never repudiated any industrial action our members have been involved in. I set up a £35 million strike fund to make certain we can sustain our members in dispute. It is ready and waiting, and has helped win numerous victories for our members. We've had over 1,000 industrial action ballots over the last three years and won almost all of them. That's the confidence the strike fund gives. The mere fact that we are willing, as a union, to set aside so much money to fight for justice in the workplace is enough to bring many employers to their senses. Smart companies quickly realise the game is up. As I recalled to delegates at our 2018 conference, 'money doesn't talk, it swears' (as Bob Dylan once wrote). It's a message well understood in the boardrooms of the UK and the world.

In the past, workers were forced to abandon industrial action when the money ran out and public donations weren't enough to feed their families. These included the miners, the print unions at Wapping, the dockers and others. But unions have learned from those terrible experiences and have built up strike funds to ensure it no longer happens.

Of course, for workers on strike, these funds do not replace their pay, nor do they keep them on the picket line without any loss. But they do keep them going. For example, the civil service union PCS asks activists to contribute a small amount to their fund each month. There were major strikes a few years ago at the National Museum of Wales and at London's National Gallery, both of which relied heavily on strike pay from that fund.

Unions use their collective voice to seek leverage. This is one of the essential strengths of the trade union movement. Unite set up an organising and leverage department in 2005 in order to develop a strategy for widening our traditional collective action, going beyond our key terms, conditions and demands in the workplace to sector-based campaigning. As a consequence of its successes, our bespoke form of leverage has been the subject of many attempts to declare it illegal. But how do you leverage an employer? What happens when everyday relations between an employer and their workers turn hostile?

To give one example, in the mid-2000s we identified the top four supermarkets that were refusing to accept a minimum standards agreement for agency labour. We decided to find out everything we could about each of them: how they operated, their emerging markets, and so on. By doing that we were able to lever them into the negotiating room. This was not about organising actions such as boycotts, choking supply chains or demonstrating outside AGMs; it was rather a tactic of 'following the money'. We committed ourselves to understanding everything there was to know about each company, just as they do when they make takeover and acquisition decisions. We did this so that when they told us they couldn't afford a pay rise for our members because their margins were so small, we would know the truth. Leverage will never be a substitute for strike action, but it can be an extremely effective additional weapon in our armoury.

When leverage and strike funds are put together, this demonstrates just how powerful a union can be in its determination to secure workers a bigger share of the profits they work so hard to achieve. People have said that other general secretaries would not have taken the risks that I have with leverage. That may be true, but plenty of other unions have come to us, including sister unions in America and parts of Europe, wanting to adopt our model. The most important aspect of what we are doing is that we are not scared to lose, because it is fear that mutes people.

Leverage works alongside organising. It is important to explain that organising is not just recruitment. Back in 1998, the TUC set up its Organising Academy headed by the now TUC general secretary, Frances O'Grady, based on similar models in the US and Australia. It worked on the thinking that organisation needed to be built into a union's recruitment strategy, in response to a dramatic decline in union membership. A cadre of union organisers were brought in from the participating unions and sent on a twelve-month training programme designed to give them the skills and experience needed to deliver effective organising campaigns and to empower members and activists in the workplace. It was described at the time as an attempt to rediscover the 'social movement' origins of the trade unions.

My union was not involved with the Academy initially, but we did join up after Tony Woodley became general secretary. He bravely created our own organising department, with a more muscular bottom-up strategy, putting organisers into workplaces, identifying leaders, and then moving to the collective sign-up of thousands of people to the union. We focused in particular on anti-union and non-unionised 'greenfield' sites in the construction and manufacturing sectors. This way, we believed, the power lay with those workers who, organised in their workplace, could win on the issues that needed addressing. In the first few years we gained 69,000 members just through this form of organising.

So, while organising does recruit people, it is primarily about building leadership structures and collective membership, so that all workers who join understand that being a part of the union reaps benefits. The work unions are doing in the precarious gig economy is a perfect demonstration of this. While the gig workers' voice is missing in so many of the debates about the relevance of trade unions to the modern world of work, we are empowering and giving a voice to those very same workers.

Unions give us strength, together, to fight bad bosses. And the results are palpable. In 2018, the Centre for Policy Studies chief, Robert Colville, claimed that unions showed a lack of gratitude to the government for 'lifting' the cap on public sector pay.[6] He accused the left and the unions, singling me out in particular, of using sleight-of-hand tactics to obscure evidence that public sector pay has been growing faster than wages in the private sector. 'You don't see Len McCluskey going on TV and weeping crocodile tears for the underpaid private sector', he complained.

Colville was blatantly ignoring the fact that I have spent all my working life fighting for decent pay and equality across all sectors of the economy, and that my industrial background has been predominantly in the private sector. Furthermore, his claim itself obscured a simple truth: union members in the private sector are getting better pay deals than those in non-unionised firms, multiple times a year. To give just a few examples: over a thousand workers at Pirelli Tyres received an inflation-busting 5 per cent pay increase. Unite and GMB members at the Rosyth dockyard, working for Babcock engineering, won a pay rise of at least £2,000, a 7.2–9.2 per cent increase. Negotiations between union and management at 2 Sisters Food Group hammered out a 9.3 per cent pay deal. Low-paid Mitie workers at Sellafield in Cumbria – security guards, cleaners, and vending, laundry and environmental operatives – won an historic pay rise of 55 pence an hour after a long and difficult dispute which, memorably, featured women strikers Zumba dancing on the picket lines. Clearly, being in a trade union benefits working people, including in the private sector. Our members consistently see a pay premium – we call it the union dividend.

And it's not just me who says that. Andy Haldane, chief economist of the Bank of England, confirmed that union membership is associated with higher pay for workers of between 10 and 15 per cent.

Gaining recognition, stopping people getting the sack, sorting out their grievances, getting them a pay rise. It gives enormous satisfaction. Going back to members with a good offer and it being accepted – it makes you think, 'That's what my union is there for.' My son Ian is now a union officer and he was overjoyed and emotional when, in one week, he stopped two people getting the sack. That's why he's a trade unionist.

Unity also comes from learning together. Nelson Mandela once said: 'Education is the most powerful weapon which you can use to change the world.' Knowledge is indeed power. No wonder the establishment has always opposed the advance of education and tried to undermine its importance. Trade unionism has always been about learning as well as raising standards in the workplace and elsewhere. Learning gives people literacy, numeracy and other skills, and ultimately helps to give working people a voice.

When I was a young shop steward I went on numerous training courses, then mainly run by the TUC, in order to equip myself better to fulfil the role effectively. Education gives you confidence, the most important word I have ever come across in the movement. It is vital as a trade unionist to feel confident about the issues we face, and when people are empowered with knowledge they can fight back.

Unions have always been educators. The very first paid trade union officers, in the 1800s, were called organiser educators. It was understood even then that until working-class people gained some confidence, it would not be possible to engender a sense of: 'I am better than this, we can do better than this, we can make our working lives better than this.' More recently, the 1974 Labour government introduced union learning reps and time off work for education. The TUC seized on this, launching a massive, progressive and professional trade union education campaign, which was a seismic change in relation to what had come before.

The electrical trade union provided basic technical competence training and examinations, issuing workers with a 'passport' that enabled them to go onto a building site. In this context, I am reminded of the black-cab driver who once took me to Liverpool Lime Street station. He told me that through his membership of Unite he was studying for a professional driver NVQ qualification. Unions, then, are educating working-class people in a way that the state has consistently failed to do, and doing so in a way that is more accessible, of better quality and cheaper than the private sector. Providing such courses for members to gain professional qualifications continues to be a growing area of our work today.

As a consequence we're providing what employers need, and what society needs. Unqualified workers can be a major threat to safety, environmental and quality standards. Take, for example, the great oil tanker dispute of 2012, in which Unite members raised concerns about training and safety standards being driven down by a fracturing of the industry into smaller suppliers, and contracts being awarded on the basis of cost not quality. This led to the introduction of a similar passport for trained drivers, which has been highly successful.

But unions can also offer courses beyond professional training. As so many of our members left school at the earliest possible age, they are eager to join these courses, written for them by professionals, delivered by full-time tutors, free through state funding, and which employers are compelled to allow them to attend. Of course, these classes are functional rather than political, but trade union education is about more than learning to be a good shop steward, an effective health and safety rep, or whatever role the student wants to fulfil. It is also about understanding the political context in which those roles operate. We do not ram political theory down anyone's throat, but we do give a political context that allows them to exercise their roles properly.

On all our courses we use very modern teaching methods to ensure they are relevant. There is no point in being a great employment lawyer, with lots of stories about case victories to tell, if those stories do not resonate with students' working lives. Trade union education should not be a test of how much people know, but a way of helping them to do their job better. A great example of this is Louisa Bull, now a Unite national officer, who left school at seventeen and went to work as a Fleet Street clerical (as they were known) for the *Daily Telegraph*. She was a shop steward by the age of nineteen, and got her political education 'on the streets', as she puts it. By the time her daughter went to university, Louisa was a full-time union official, keen to 'put a frame' around the work she was doing:

I lacked the political theory and academic knowledge to give me a proper understanding of what I was doing in representing members. There was then a part-time industrial relations, economics and labour law course at Birkbeck College, London, and the union paid the fees for me and another officer to enrol, along with time off to attend courses. After graduating I was selected as the TUC's candidate for a three-month trade union programme at Harvard University in the US, which gave me a more global perspective.

There, among her tutors, was Noam Chomsky, the great American political activist and linguist.

Jobs develop people, but undoubtedly trade unions develop them more deeply and roundly, and give them a voice through the many and varied educational opportunities they offer. It's actually quite difficult to know how a new generation of trade unionists would develop without this union commitment to learning.

4

A WORLD WITHOUT UNIONS

Policies are designed to undermine working class organiza-
tion and the reason is not only the unions fight for workers'
rights, but they also have a democratizing effect. These are
institutions in which people without power can get together,
support one another, learn about the world, try out their
ideas, initiate programs, and that is dangerous.

Noam Chomsky

What would a world without unions look like? Are unions
still relevant in a changing world, in which the robots are
coming for so many of our good jobs, and may even go
for what's left of the rest? Our history shows that unions
are the barometers of such changes. We see these kinds of
development at their earliest stages. We hear our members'
anecdotes as events happen. We do the research to uncover
what is really going on. Without us, workplaces today

would be dangerous, deadly and largely devoid of decent jobs. Unregulated, low-paid, insecure, zero-hour contract and agency jobs with long hours would be practically all that remained. Yes, such jobs now dominate our service sector economy, but without unions they would exist with none of the rights and protections either already won for workers, or currently being fought for.

What are the victories won by unions that have made our working lives safer and fairer?

Karl Marx, in his great critique of how the capitalist system works, *Capital*, wrote about the struggle for the 'normal working day' that brought about the Factory Acts. He described how capital, over centuries, had extended the working day not just to its natural limit, but beyond (so that even the definitions of day and night became confused). Many of the reforms to post-industrial-revolution working conditions and workers' rights were achieved by the struggle of the emerging labour movement. They were secured through industrial disputes, or by working with progressive Labour governments, or by exploiting the opportunities the law provides to fight injustices. Anti-union laws throughout history have left employers holding most of the cards, but the law has also been a weapon in our armoury that can help give workers a voice.

Trade unions and their lawyers have pursued most of the test cases that established and developed the laws around health and safety at work, both before and since the 1974 Health and Safety at Work Act. For example, it was unions who brought the first ever successful case for asbes-tos-related-disease compensation in the UK to the House of Lords in 1972, and they have been involved in every significant case around the law of asbestos compensation since then. Unions have supported hundreds of workers and their families who have developed asbestos-related diseases as a result of exposure at work or in childhood.

That is not all. Without both the industrial and politi-cal work undertaken by trade unions, there would be no laws governing maximum working hours, no working-at-height regulations, no personal protective equipment, no lifting and manual handling regulations, no sick pay, no right to paid rest breaks. I could go on, and as dry as some of these terms may seem – and as much as they might bring about howls of 'health and safety gone mad' from the *Daily Mail* – they make all our working lives safer.

Our legal battles have also protected employment rights: equal pay, the national minimum wage, agency workers' rights, pension rights, family friendly policies, maternity and paternity leave, holiday pay, the right not to be discrim-inated against, the right to time off work for trade union activities, the right to be accompanied by a trade union rep to grievance and disciplinary hearings. These are all rights that if you were starting work today, you'd simply take for granted (though not in the gig economy).

For example, in 2017 the Supreme Court confirmed that the coalition Tory–Liberal Democrat government was wrong to deny working people access to justice by imposing fees for employment tribunals (ET) in 2010. It was a case pursued by Unison but was a victory for all workers, and particularly for equality and for the restoration of a semblance of balance in the workplace. Tribunal fees required anyone who felt they had been dealt an injustice at work to pay up to £1,200 to make a claim. The result was a shocking drop in sex, race and disability discrimination claims: nearly 80 per cent fewer ET cases were brought over three years. This allowed discrimination at work to flourish unchecked – a gift to bad bosses from the political party that claims to be the friend of working people. And even now the Ministry of Justice is considering how to bring fees back.[1]

Elsewhere, establishing in the courts that Uber drivers are 'workers', and therefore entitled to basic rights such as the minimum wage, holiday pay, sick pay and parental leave, was a fantastic victory for the GMB. Unite, meanwhile, won a landmark legal victory forcing employers to include voluntary overtime in holiday pay calculations.[2] These are ground-breaking successes that undoubtedly level the playing field a little, but they do not end exploitative employment practices on their own. Nor do they, in isolation, empower workers or provide collective or equal rights. Legal action doesn't replace the work that unions must do, organising in workplaces to drive out unfairness and injustice.

Twice we successfully defeated a High Court challenge by Argos intended to quash our industrial action, begun to start the fight back against the restrictions placed on unions by the Trade Union Act. That action did not get rid of the Act, but it did demonstrate how trade union legal strategies have an essential part to play in our continued fight on behalf of our members, and how our legal work is now more integrated with our industrial activity than it ever has been.

Pursuing these strategies also won compensation of over £10 million for blacklisted workers in the building industry. Obviously, no sum can overcome the injustice done to those workers, whose lives were wrecked by firms who denied them work on account of their trade unionism and by the police and security services, who we now know, as a result of the 'spycops' inquiry, were also involved in the blacklisting of workers on an industrial scale.[3] However, securing compensation has been a big step towards righting that wrong. Unions continue to fight for such victims, but only a separate public inquiry will reveal the full truth of the scandal.

In landmark litigation we have established that it is unlawful for companies to offer pay rises to those who leave a union. We successfully challenged British Airway's attempts to financially punish the mixed fleet members who took strike action. BA was forced finally to concede that it had to resolve the sanctions issue and compensate our members.

Nowhere has the integration of legal and industrial action been more visible during the Birmingham bins dispute, where members went on strike against pay cuts imposed by a Labour council who had bullied both workers and their union, and had reneged on a settlement reached at ACAS. Unite secured an injunction to stop the local authority making the workers redundant. This legal action was key in forcing the employer back to its senses.

Demonstrating solidarity with fellow workers in dispute is a fundamental principle of trade unionism, and it is appalling that in twenty-first-century Britain we risk losing our jobs for doing it. The International Labour Organisation (ILO) has repeatedly condemned the UK for its non-compliance with international law due to its excessive restrictions on trade union rights. But history has shown that we are not incapable of getting around the anti-union laws designed to weaken us. We should be more prepared to challenge the law, rather than just accepting that certain actions are illegal.

The film *Nae Pasaran* tells the story of the Rolls-Royce workers of East Kilbride who defied Pinochet by refusing to work on the Chilean air force's Hawker Hunter jet fighter engines that had been sent to their site for maintenance.[4] If workers tried to take similar solidarity action today, their union's funds could be seized, because the definition of a trade dispute has been so narrowed. This is why John McDonnell's pledge that a Labour government will restore the right to strike in solidarity with those in struggle in other countries, along with repealing all of Thatcher's anti-unions laws, is so welcome.[5]

In the past, especially during the Thatcher period, unions did not have the leadership to resist the concerted assault on their powers, designed to drive a wedge between the unions and their members. When New Labour came to power in 1997 it did very little to restore trade union rights. But we have to be willing to challenge the status quo. When I became general secretary, I was successful in removing the wording 'within the law' from Unite's rulebook. I did that because I knew there might come a time when we had to act outside the law, and I did not want to be in breach of my own union's rules, nor refuse to support a group of workers in dispute on account of bad laws.[6]

The last thing workers in dispute need is their union coming up with excuses for why it can't support them. We have to be prepared to stand firm, even if we're facing a serious attack, such as being taken to court. So far that has not happened to Unite, even though we've never repudiated, but we have to be careful that we're not always fighting the power of the state. Nevertheless, I do believe it's important to send a message that, in defending our members, we're not going to be restricted by laws that are unfair. We sometimes face injunctions intended to prevent strikes, but we can play the employers at their own game, with the law.

There's another landmark case that demonstrates how, with a little imagination, unions can exert economic pressure on employers without butting up against the law.[7] In 1993 the T&G could not prevent the sacking of workers

by Middlebrook Mushrooms, but when the sacked workers took to the streets and leafleted outside supermarkets, urging shoppers not to buy the firm's mushrooms,
they were not acting illegally. The courts confirmed that
targeting the public, not the employer, was perfectly fine.
Similarly, members of the train drivers' union ASLEF are
renowned for their ability to stop the trains. It's difficult to
run a railway when the drivers all have flu.

And then there are the consequences for employers
of the precarious employment models they so love. The
hundred or so fast-food couriers who brought parts of
central London to a standstill in 2018, by riding en masse
on their scooters and bikes in demand of an increased
minimum payment for deliveries, did not need to bother
with the balloting requirements of the Trade Union Act.[8]
This is a reminder that if workers are without rights, they
are without responsibilities too.

The Durham Miners' Gala each July is a highlight of my
year. It is a wonderful, vibrant celebration of trade union
values and community spirit. It also provides the opportunity to survey not just the devastation of our former mining
communities, but the widespread deindustrialisation of
cities and towns throughout the country. This is the story
of our movement from the 1980s to today, and the impact
it has had on trade unions, and the cumulative effect of that
on the economy and nature of work, is why we should be
trade unionists. As well as having a legal role, the unions

have a political responsibility to participate in debates over the state of the economy and the nation.

Strikes during the 1970s, especially in the so-called Winter of Discontent of 1978/9, were, and still are, blamed for wrecking productivity. Thatcher famously claimed that unions were 'the enemy within', that 'monopoly trade unions have immense potential for destruction and can inflict severe damage and hardship'.[9] And she went on to crush the strikes by the miners, the dockers and others.

The real enemy to productivity and growth, however, is not the trade unions but short-termism in the British economy. Instead of looking long term to sustained growth, ten or twenty years down the line, and including unions as key economic players in that, we are saddled with anti-union, anti-worker laws that have made us the worst protected workforce in Western Europe. As a result, consecutive administrations have focused on how quickly they can extract wealth; an approach that has put hedge fund managers in the driving seat and driven the country to the edge of ruin.

The destruction of British manufacturing, in particular heavy industry, began in the 1980s with Thatcher's neoliberal economics and her determination to break the unions, alongside Ronald Reagan's deregulating assault on industry and the creation of 'liberal' conditions for finance to operate on a more global stage. We tend to forget that Thatcher went for the steel industry first, before going after the miners, the printers and then the dockers. The first national strike by steel workers for more than fifty years took place in 1980, over pay and the threat of plant closures at the loss-making nationalised industry. Although a deal was struck after fourteen weeks, the government appointed Ian MacGregor as British Steel chairman to drive through a savage rationalisation programme. By the end of the year, three major steelworks had closed with the loss of 20,000 jobs. Between 1979 and 1981, total employment in the industry halved. In 1988, when British Steel was profitable again, it was swiftly sold off as part of Thatcher's privatisation programme.

The Tories' successive waves of anti-union legislation began with the 1980 Employment Act, followed by the 1982 Employment Act, the Trade Union Act 1984, the Public Order Act 1986 and a further Employment Act in 1988. The measures included restricting the right to strike, making secondary action unlawful, criminalising some types of picketing, ending the closed shop, undercutting worker protections, and reducing the capacity of trade unions to organise and to conduct their own business in line with their own rules.

Thatcher may have started this, but successive governments allowed labour, as a commodity, to be discounted in the drive towards a flexible, service sector economy. New Labour was happy to allow this swing away from manufacturing to continue, in favour of Private Finance Initiatives (PFIs) and the fragmentation of work. Its leadership was part of a national consensus that was willing to embrace a globalised free market, a deregulated financial sector and a flexible labour market.

New Labour refused to recognise the economic impact of not freeing the unions from Thatcher's shackles. Tony Blair remained true to his disgraceful boast that under his government anti-union legislation would continue to be the most restrictive in Europe. 'We will still have the most restrictive union laws in the Western world, and it will stay that way', he told the *Sun* during the 1997 election campaign.[10] It is shameful that neither the Blair nor Brown governments recognised that the only way to deliver more and better public services was with the help of a vibrant manufacturing sector.

The impact? One million manufacturing jobs were lost under New Labour. Manufacturing's share of UK economic output had stood at 27 per cent in 1970, but by 2017 it was just 10 per cent. In every other major European economy – France, Spain, Italy and Germany (with 23 per cent) – manufacturing has a higher share. Service sector output in the UK has risen by 97 per cent over the last thirty years; by 2017 it constituted 79 per cent of the economy, up from 69 per cent in 1990. By September 2018, services accounted for 83 per cent of workforce jobs.

During the 1970s, when the trade unions were strong, living standards took great strides forward for millions of people. But the dramatic changes the Tories made to collective bargaining during the 1980s made it much more difficult to organise workers on a sectoral basis, so that by

1990 collective bargaining coverage had fallen to 55 per cent from around 70 per cent in 1980. By the turn of the millennium, only one in three workers were covered by a collective bargaining agreement.

More recently, the GMB was offered a recognition deal by a gig economy employer. Since it did not include a collective bargaining agreement, they turned it down. This was the right thing to do. The ability of trade unions to negotiate on behalf of their members means they can make a difference. Collective bargaining is what the insecure and gig economy needs more than anything else, to enable unions to organise the workforce more effectively, to raise pay and conditions, and to stop unscrupulous employers in the sector competing by means of undercutting. Without collective bargaining, union recognition amounts to little more than a dialogue between a powerful boss and a tame staff association, allowing representation on some matters but not on the most essential. It is not quite a world without unions, but it is not far off.

It is no accident that workers' share of GDP (Gross Domestic Product) in Britain has fallen from a high of almost 70 per cent in the 1970s to around 50 per cent today. Any A-level economics student could tell you the devastating impact that has on an economy. And it is a direct result of deindustrialisation and deunionisation.

There has been no coherent industrial strategy in Britain to ensure trade unions, government and industry work together since Tony Benn's 'Alternative Economic

Strategy' of 1975. Yet how we respond to the changing nature of work – to decasualised, precarious employment, and to the twin challenges of automation and digitalisation – is critical to the country's debate around productivity.

In 2015 I wrote to the then chancellor, George Osborne, after he said Britain must address its poor productivity, and that we did not export, train, invest, manufacture or build enough. I agreed with him, and urged a dialogue between all parties on how to address this challenge – a dialogue that had to include trade unions as representatives of millions of employees. Osborne had also confirmed the government's intention to announce a 'productivity plan'. I welcomed this, but said it was imperative that workers and their trade unions were part of any plan to address the UK's poor productivity.

I did not get a response, of course, and, inevitably, UK productivity figures continue to reflect Osborne's and successive Conservative governments' refusal to adopt an active industrial strategy, engage with unions, and support manufacturing.[11]

Analysis by the *Financial Times* in 2018 found that, in the previous two years, the increase in low-paid jobs had held back productivity growth in the UK.[12] Employment trends were behind this, and it confirmed what unions have been warning of for many years. The labour market is fast changing around us and the pace of that change is astonishing. We know there are areas in which the UK can be a world leader, including in renewables and electric vehicle

battery technology, but it needs political will and government investment, both of which have been severely lack-
ing for decades.

For trade unions, an industrial strategy means building a strong economy that genuinely works for all, underpinned by secure employment, decent pay and conditions,
protections against the exploitation of migrant and other
workers, and safeguards for the future of our members'
jobs and communities.

Unite, for one, has mapped out industrial and political
responses to automation and digitalisation, offering advice
to negotiators and discussing the issues with our shop
stewards so that our members have a say in their workplaces. Yet the role of unions was absent from the 2017
government Green Paper on industrial strategy, exposing
what I believe is the fatal weakness in the government's
approach: the absence of the collective voice of working
people.[13] Trade unions know how to increase productivity
and how to address investment questions. Britain's most
productive sectors have included car manufacturing, aero-
space and other engineering sectors. These are the areas
now hugely suffering because of the Tories' disastrous
handling of Brexit. However, there is a high level of union
density in these sectors, and trade unions working in partnership with employers have been central to the improvements secured.

This does not entail a return to the union–employer
partnership arrangements that became popular in the

1990s, which effectively saw union leaders swallowing the bosses' neoliberal dogma. Those were bad years for me, during which, to be honest, I lost pride in my union. There was a dangerous slide towards mediocrity, towards what I see as 'business unionism' – as opposed to class-based trade unionism – focusing only on the immediate economic interests of union members (as important as they are) and ignoring the wider issues in society. Unions must be genuine partners in industry, just as they are in Germany. As I have said, 95 per cent of our time as trade unionists is spent resolving often complex issues that an employer cannot deal with on their own. Unions are central to our democracy, not an obstacle to it.

Take the voluntary three-day week introduced at Alexander Dennis, the Falkirk-based coach manufacturer, which in 2013 was struggling financially. It was union shop stewards who identified the change needed to stop the company slipping back into the administration from which it had been rescued in 2004.[14] Similarly, when Tory ministers herald the success of the UK motor industry, they seem to forget that it was trade unionists who ensured it was so. The Vauxhall plant at Ellesmere Port on Merseyside remained open after our shop stewards concluded difficult negotiations with General Motors. And when the company reneged on its promises and cut and ran, we engaged with the new owner, PSA, to secure commitments for investment.

After PSA announced it would be investing £170 million in its Luton plant to bring a new Vauxhall van model to the

UK, creating 450 new jobs, I paid tribute to the dedicated workforce there. In 2018 – in the midst of Honda's decision to leave the UK, Ford's to close its Bridgend plant, and PSA's warnings that a new model at Ellesmere Port could be imperilled by a no-deal Brexit – Jaguar Land Rover (JLR) announced its investment in a new electric vehicle. To secure that investment, production workers at JLR's Castle Bromwich plant in the West Midlands agreed to move to working a condensed week, offering them greater work–life balance, while giving the car maker greater flexibility. This agreement was testament to the skill and hard work of members and shop stewards.

The UK government's attitude towards trade unions is critical in dealing with the challenges that lie ahead. I visited the Rolls-Royce car plant at Goodwood and the Mini plant in Oxford on the same day – both British cars owned by BMW. The plant managers were both German engineers and I asked them the same question: 'what difference do you see between Germany and the UK?' Their identical answers: 'In the UK you don't seem to take manufacturing seriously.'

On the shopfloor at Oxford, the managing director said to me:

Lenny, here we are producing an iconic British car, in an iconic British plant, with British workers. There's a warehouse with 600 robots working alongside your members and the robots are all made in Germany.

Why? Because I can't get them made here in the UK. In my plants in Germany, the robots are made in Germany. And not only that, they make them around the corner to the car factory, so if anything goes wrong we can easily solve the problem. Here in the UK, I'd love our robots to be British built, but no one is making them.

That comment encapsulates our country's response to the changing world of work and the rise of the robots. Should automation just work for the bosses, or should it work for all of us? How can automation provide us with decent jobs, and how can the fundamental role of unions ensure that it does?

RBS, the bank that was at the epicentre of Britain's economic crash in 2008, and had to be bailed out by taxpayers, is cutting staff and branch costs by replacing human employees with digital ones. A 2018 episode of Radio 4's *In Business* included this alarming comment by the presenter, after she had been introduced to Cora, RBS's 'digital human' customer advisor: 'Unlike human employees, Cora doesn't get sick, she doesn't need maternity leave or holidays, and she doesn't even get paid.'[15]

It struck me, on hearing this chilling representation of the potential impact of new technology on jobs, that this approach is not far removed from the treatment that so many real, non-digital humans experience at the hands of many service sector employers today. RBS's development of Cora is so entirely concentrated on cutting costs, wrapped up in a customer-experience focus, that there is an almost callous disregard for those whose jobs the highly programmed avatar will replace.

But Cora wasn't developed in a vacuum. There was a significant development team behind her. The speed and nature of technological advances in recent years – leading to this new wave of automation and digitalisation, the so-called fourth industrial revolution – cast a long shadow. The replacement of workers by robots is an issue facing all areas of manufacturing and the service sector. According to a 2016 World Economic Forum survey, an estimated 1.6 million manufacturing and production jobs will be lost globally due to automation by 2020.[16] Unite's own research has identified more than 650,000 members working in sectors where they are at high risk of losing their jobs through automation, and over 231,700 of these by 2035.[17]

But there's no reason why workers shouldn't get their fair share of the eye-watering amount of money there is to be made from automation. The Labour Party's 'Build it in Britain' policy is therefore most welcome. It recognises that the UK was once the workshop of the world, but that successive governments have allowed our economy to swing towards the service sector. We are now more a warehouse than a workshop. Certainly we still make things, but we significantly lag behind competitor nations in the production of components, not least electric car batteries, which will be essential to the future of the auto industry, the jewel in our country's manufacturing crown.[18]

I have been accused by some of wanting to halt progress. When I tweeted about the need to 'build things here again', several responders charged that the actions of unions will ensure we never do. I was told that we want to rebuild the dark satanic mills of our industrial past, along with the working and living conditions they came with. To this I can only respond that, if we are talking about satanic mills and nineteenth-century workhouses, then we need look no further than the warehouses of large-scale retail operations like Amazon and Sports Direct, who have rebuilt the dreaded walls of the factories of yore and reproduced their living and working conditions.

In such places, wages remain at the minimum legally payable. Terms, employment conditions and rights are threadbare. It is impossible to dismiss the scandal of Amazon workers forced to sleep in tents near the Dunfermline warehouse – unable to afford to commute and terrified of the consequences of being late for shifts – as the price of progress.[19] We will never forget the tragic death of the DPD courier who missed medical appointments to avoid the firm's £150 daily penalties if he did not find cover for his shift.[20] As trade unionists, we must not forget the past, but neither should we want to restore it. Instead we need to build for an industrial technological future, particularly if that future is outside of Europe.

Ahead of his 2017 budget, I called on the then chancellor, Philip Hammond, to establish a Brexit support fund to target investment where it was most urgently needed. This would, I suggested, free up sites for new technologies, including the development and manufacture of electric batteries and robots. As well as supporting re-skilling and talent creation, this would involve the government taking a public stake, not just in preventing big business from controlling the fund, but in controlling our country's economic develop. It would also send a message to manufacturers that the UK is a place to do business, in fairness and with confidence.

Trade unions are the largest voluntary organisations in our society, and yet we are cut out of the most vital conversation of our times by the government. Theresa May's claim, during her marathon House of Commons session defending her doomed Brexit deal, that the unions had been involved throughout the process was quite simply wrong. The calls she made to union leaders just days before her deal was overwhelmingly defeated were the first time she'd ever spoken to us, though some of us did then meet her and talks continued with her government for a while, for all they achieved. May's contact with us was two-and-a-half years too late.

Automation should offer the prospect of shorter working weeks, with no loss of pay, or become the gateway to a nationwide programme of re-skilling and up-skilling for existing workers. It should create new training and high-quality apprenticeship schemes for jobs in programming and operating the robots, and in the development of digital humans like Cora. We need the government to take the lead in setting up a Future of Automation Commission, involving unions, employers, researchers and academics in finding workable solutions to automation, seeking to understand both the opportunities it offers and the threats it poses.

5
WE ARE FAMILY

Trade unions are a force for good – a force for a more equal society.

Jeremy Corbyn

A few years ago, I was walking through the Labour Party conference centre thinking about the fringe meeting I was on my way to. A colleague asked why I was humming the theme tune to *The Archers*. I didn't realise I was, but it got us into an interesting discussion. Why are there no trade unionists in today's soap operas?

Perhaps uniquely, *Brookside*, set in Liverpool in the 1980s, reflected the trade union principles of some of the inhabitants of the Close. The great and brave real-life trade unionist Ricky Tomlinson, as Bobby Grant, fought hard for his members' rights in his workplace, and brought his trade unionism right back into his community, albeit a cul-de-sac of middle-class semis, where people got buried under patios. But where are the trade unionists in the communities of *EastEnders*? *The Archers*' David Archer has dabbled with the National Farmers' Union, but that's an employer's organisation, whatever it may call itself. And *Coronation Street*? I remember the first knicker strike in the late 1970s, followed by the walkout of workers at the underwear factory owned by bad boss Mike Baldwin. There was no mention of a union, despite there being an appropriate one for the sector. Over the years, strikes have continued to pop up in the *Coronation Street* storyline, but more recently with an apparent total absence of trade union involvement, or an industrial reason for taking action.

Can anyone believe that within the communities that soap operas depict there are no union members? Do scriptwriters think that the people whose stories they tell don't have political convictions and don't bring them home after work? The depiction of strikes at the *Coronation Street* factory reveals how the show once reflected the working-class community it stood for. Now its characters, although they still live in that environment, seem detached from such a reality. The conversations they have are more about consumerism than collectivism. Where are the chats in the pub, or the café, about the impact of what an employer has announced that day and how best to deal with it?

But working-class communities still exist and the role of trade unions within them remains important. They are still at the forefront of the battle against austerity and poverty, even if the days of mass union membership are gone. We used to have labour and trade union social clubs, when people lived in the communities where they worked. They were a source of great solidarity, unity and support. If someone was in difficulty, that's where they would turn.

Unions remain central to communities where there are still large concentrations of, for example, railway workers – such as those working at the big depots in Doncaster and Crewe – and they provide a service, a focal point and an identity. I spoke at a May Day rally at the Doncaster Trades club in 2018, which was a fantastic resource for the community and local businesses, for social events and political meetings. And in a sense that reflects the origins of trade unions in the late seventeenth and early eighteenth centuries, as underground trade and friendly societies. They tended to be locally based, and concerned with providing friendly social benefits.[1]

Perhaps it's because workplaces are increasingly separated from the communities they once served that we perceive trade unions as no longer having any impact on them. After all, many of us now travel for hours to get to work, particularly in our cities, because wages have not kept up with house prices and workers cannot afford to live near their workplaces any more. We do the same in reverse at the end of the day, day after day, at huge cost and discomfort, given the state of our privatised railways.

Take a car factory like Ellesmere Port. There is no central point any more because the workers live across

Merseyside and beyond. And, of course, lifestyles change, and different types of organisations and activities take over as the focus of people's working and leisure lives.

But, returning to my experience on the Liverpool docks, I know exactly what they, and the trade union values I learned there, taught me: solidarity, the importance of the collective, working-class identity, and why we stick together.

I was brought up on community and it helped to form my politics. Growing up in Liverpool was full of happy times. I did not grow up in the slums, but I did live in a poor part of the City, in a two-up-two-down house. We were always playing games in the street, whether football, cricket or, when Wimbledon was on, tennis with makeshift rackets and no net. And there were many happy Saturday mornings spent in the Commodore Picture House, where we paid a few pence to get in.

After I took the job on the docks, I walked down Bankhall and Bankfield Street every day. We called it the Golden Mile because it had five pubs, two betting shops, a nightclub and a greasy spoon café. The area was alive and vibrant, with so many different characters. And that's where my politics started to take proper shape.

Today there is not a single pub or betting shop, the club has gone and there is no greasy spoon. Bankhall and Bankfield are deserted, a shadow of what they were. There has been no development post-deindustrialisation; the road that leads down to the dock, once full of lorries, is empty. It makes me really sad.

When I was growing up I saw how, outside of work, trade unionists lived in their communities. Trade unions were part of everyday life in Liverpool, and whenever there were issues in the community it was often union members who were at the forefront of any campaign for change. People extended the solidarity they had in work into the community. This is the great characteristic of the working class: those wonderful values of solidarity and community spirit.

When I look at the now-devastated mining communities of Britain, I am reminded of the damage inflicted by forty years of deindustrialisation, which has broken the links between trade unions and communities. The decimation of our traditional manufacturing industries, and the introduction of anti-union laws, have gone hand in hand with the decline in trade union membership. This fracturing has undoubtedly resulted in the decline of community cohesion, and the impact of austerity in those towns that have lost their industries has been far harsher as a result, leading to a sense of hopelessness, of being let down and left behind.

As research by Hope not Hate has shown,[2] and as unions have long warned, this creates an anger that racist and far-right groups and political parties seek to exploit, in order to spread hate and division. I saw this early on, when I got into physical fights with the National Front on the streets of Liverpool and Birkenhead, and when I heard and saw the ugly face of racism on our football terraces. The far right breeds in communities and areas that have been abandoned by the political elite. And that is why politics matters, and why trade unionism matters.

Throughout the 1990s and 2000s, after I became a national secretary and then assistant general secretary for the T&G and later Unite, I increasingly wanted to do something to try to reconnect unions and communities. I will admit I was nostalgic for the sort of collective community spirit I experienced on the Liverpool docks; but while we cannot go back to the past, I believe we can rebuild it through trade unions.

There's no doubt that Margaret Thatcher added fuel to the fire by destroying working-class jobs and communities. Take, for example, Vauxhall Road in Liverpool. It was once full of factories, but the decline started in the late 1970s as changes in global trade led to reduced demand for the goods and materials exported from the docks. Thatcher had no interest in reversing that decline and so, by 1982, the factories had mostly closed, throwing whole families out of work. But what struck me, when I took on the national role in my union in 1990 and began travelling to every part of the country, was that even after Thatcher's ravages, unions remained a part of everyday life in Liverpool and other (mainly northern) cities. But it was not like that everywhere, and I saw directly how attitudes to unions had changed and how the decline in membership was a direct result of the devastation of our traditional manufacturing industries.

Two things hit home about the workers I encountered everywhere: the pride they took in their jobs and the products or services they offered; and the class values and culture that remained. Wherever I went I still found a belief in community spirit and solidarity, in helping your fellow man or woman, and this helped to strengthen my own belief in our class identity.

So I wanted to recognise and re-establish, as far as possible, and in the absence of a supportive government, how things were before our workplaces began to be closed down. To reconstitute the working class as a force. I also wanted to show that, while the primary function of trade unions is to represent workers in work, we are not vested interest organisations, concerned only to protect jobs and secure better pay for our members. Our members live in their communities, they have neighbours with problems. Why shouldn't they be able to join the union family too?

And so, in setting up Unite Community in 2012, we opened our union's doors to those not in work, inviting them to join the union family for just 50 pence a week. For me, this was as much about the fact that our members in work were going home to communities that lacked the collectivism they enjoyed in work, as it was about how those who were losing their jobs needed trade union support where they lived. With the Tories attacking working-class communities – and austerity dismantling the network of organisations that people might have turned to for help and advice, including law centres and unemployed workers' centres – I saw that these communities needed trade union support just as much as working people do in their workplaces.

Unite Community is extending our reach into marginalised communities largely deserted by politicians and established trade unionism. This has become a fundamental part of our union's political response to the Tories' aggressive agenda of cuts. It has helped to ensure that we are at the forefront of political, industrial and community opposition to austerity.

We invited not only the unemployed through our doors, but all those not in paid work, including students, pensioners, disabled people, volunteers and carers. This is undoubtedly without precedent in British trade unionism, and it adds another dimension to the union's strength, because giving people not in work the opportunity to find their own voice assists us industrially.

Like Unite, the National Union of Mineworkers (NUM) has always been a community union. Its members worked down the mines and lived in the mining villages. When local people had a problem, the union looked after them whether they were NUM members or not. The mines have gone, but that tradition is not entirely lost. The Durham Miners' Association remains a charity firmly rooted in the community, providing advice, support and representation, offering educational opportunities and cultural events, and, of course, holding the Durham Miners' Gala, the very essence of community and collectivism. Thatcher and Joseph may be long dead, but the spirit of the miners they tried to destroy lives on, and goes from strength to strength.

Unite Community was one way of trying to rebuild the community spirit that trade unionism offers, but ultimately we need a fundamental shift in the balance of power and ownership in society to really achieve it. Labour's commitment to usher in transformative change by returning key services into the hands of workers and the public through different forms of ownership is how it will be achieved.

It has been shown, time and time again, that the more highly unionised a country the more productive it is. I look to Germany, where trade unions are embraced as partners in productivity, where workers are present on boards as co-drivers of company success, and where productivity is streets ahead of the UK. This is a public ownership model very different to that first devised by Herbert Morrison, in which industries were top-down, bureaucratic public corporations, unresponsive to the needs of workers or consumers. Local, regional and commuting services are being looked at by Labour, in consultation with the unions, with a view to establishing decentralised ownership structures that will give more power to the devolved parliaments and local government.

I'm proud of Unite Community Scotland, which in 2018, working with Get Glasgow Moving, managed to get two amendments to the Scottish Parliament's Transport

Bill that could see publicly owned buses across Scotland. This is a very practical example of trade union work arising from a determination to stop a private sector company axing yet another vital service to a community.

Appropriate regulation of and representation within business is vital too, and trade unions have been working with Labour to look at changes in corporate governance and regulatory architecture, including establishing an overarching Business Commission on which workers, consumers and other community members would be represented.

Labour is also pledging to double the size of the cooperative sector. A report to John McDonnell on Alternative Models of Ownership points out that cooperative ownership can increase employment stability and production levels, as well as make firms more democratic.[3] Cooperatives cannot thrive without access to finance, any more than small- and medium-sized businesses can. But Labour's plans for an integrated industrial and investment strategy, including the setting up of national and regional investment banks and transformation funds, will, I am confident, give both expanding cooperatives and a regenerated manufacturing sector what is needed to begin the long journey back to an economy with sustained growth.

The introduction of Inclusive Ownership Funds in companies with over 250 employees – another Labour commitment – will give workers an initial ownership stake of 1 per cent, building up to 10 per cent, while workers would also make up a third of board members in both private and public companies.

While campaigning to be prime minister back in 2016, Theresa May insisted there had to be changes to the way companies were run. She pledged that 'we're going to have not just consumers on boards, but workers as well'. At the time, her words reminded me of when James Callaghan, as Labour prime minister, commissioned the Bullock Report on industrial democracy. That report promoted the idea that workers should make decisions and share responsibility and authority in the workplace. Callaghan saw the benefit of having workers on boards so that profits were diverted from investment to wages. However, in spite of strong support from the T&G, opposition from the CBI and some other unions meant that the Bullock proposals were ultimately dropped, much as May's plans were.[4]

Being a trade unionist enables us to see where value really comes from – working people. Mariana Mazzucato's book *The Value of Everything* makes the argument that it is time for different accounts of how value is created.[5] For trade unions, this means supporting and protecting the real wealth creators and putting them at the centre, not just of working lives, but of the wider issues facing our world, societies and communities, including the climate emergency.

Less than a week after the 2017 general election – an election fought by Labour on a clear anti-austerity manifesto around which the whole party united – we all watched in horror as Grenfell Tower went up in flames. We knew at the time that Grenfell was not simply a tragic accident. Just before the second anniversary of the disaster – in which seventy-two people died, including eight children – the police announced that there was no guarantee of criminal charges being brought against the guilty parties. How could that be justice?

I was at the Hillsborough stadium in 1989 on the day that ninety-six Liverpool fans lost their lives in the crush at the Leppings Lane end, and I have fought with the campaigners for justice for those victims ever since. For the families and all those affected by Hillsborough, the fight for justice, which the labour movement has been a part of, was long and hard. Twenty-seven years on, in 2016, they finally got the inquest verdict they demanded: that the victims were unlawfully killed, and that no behaviour on the part of Liverpool fans contributed to the tragedy.

Securing criminal convictions against the senior police officers and others on duty that day had been challenging. On the day after Grenfell, I said that, yet again, our class would be left to fight for our own justice, and I fear I was not wrong. The bar is still set far too high for effective prosecutions in relation to deaths through negligence. Grenfell stands as a symbol of Tory Britain, where profit is always put before people. John McDonnell was criticised for saying that those who died in the tower were murdered by years of local authority cuts, by corporate greed and uncaring capitalism, but I agree with him.

In the words of the poet Ben Okri, 'In this age of austerity, the poor die for others' prosperity.' Austerity kills.
Grenfell happened on the watch of a Tory council awash
with reserves to bribe rich voters, a council unable, or
unwilling, to protect working-class people in their homes,
and incapable of accepting responsibility for the terrible
loss of life. Kensington and Chelsea council – a symbol of
all that is rotten in Tory Britain – has still not been held to
account. And as I write this, nothing has changed. There
have been no arrests, thousands of people are still living in
buildings with deadly combustible cladding, and the Tories
are still desperate to stop the debate around Grenfell being
about austerity. Meanwhile Labour and the trade unions
– led by the Fire Brigades Union, whose members ran
towards those flames that night – continue to fight for the
truth to be told about the price we pay for cuts.

Unite alone had twenty members living in Grenfell
and, tragically, three died that night, some alongside
other members of their families. Many of our members
who survived lost family and friends. Union members
were involved from the outset, supporting residents in the
immediate humanitarian response. In those painful days
after the tragedy we provided a vital link to the wider
community, offering legal advice and representation to
many residents, in what will be a long road to justice.
Grenfell members have also received legal support from
their unions in relation to housing, welfare and employment issues arising as a direct result of the fire – injustices

that the mainstream media rarely notice. One case that stands out, though there have been many, was that of a Unite convenor in our construction sector who saved the job of a member after he had been sacked, disgracefully, for taking time off work sick because of the terrible impact of what he witnessed.

Unions raised hundreds of thousands of pounds for the Grenfell fire appeal. The £125,000 donated by our staff, branches and regions supported the immediate practical needs of our members who survived, and the families of those who did not. It paid for the funeral clothing of a family who had to bury their twelve-year-old daughter, for day-to-day clothing for many others, and for trauma counselling for members and their families suffering the severe psychological effects of the disaster.

What was left over went to extra payments for members who had finally been rehoused, to help them establish their homes again. And towards the end of 2018, we donated a memorial book to our Grenfell members, which named the branches and regions that had donated.

Telling this story is not meant as an advert for Unite Community, but I am immensely proud of what Community membership has achieved, and of the work it is doing to reconnect unions and communities. Trade unions have to be relevant to contemporary society, to the modern world of work, and to the communities people live in. But being relevant in today's communities is perhaps an even bigger challenge than remaining relevant in our changing workplaces.

The Community scheme has given thousands of people the opportunity to join a trade union, bringing them together to actively engage with, and receive advice and support on, issues that are vital to their everyday lives – such as exposing the failures and injustices of Universal Credit (UC) through national days of action and events in hundreds of towns across the country, as well as campaigning against the deeply unjust Bedroom Tax.

The impact of Community has been to put Unite at the forefront of a growing social movement. This is a movement for change that has been instrumental in reshaping politics across our nations, including the formation of the People's Assembly Against Austerity, which unites trade unions with community and other campaigning groups against cuts and privatisation in workplaces, towns and cities. It is no exaggeration to say that this community work, linking as it has to local Labour Party branches and constituencies and to other movements such as UK Uncut and Occupy, has had a significant hand in twice seeing Jeremy Corbyn elected as leader of our party.[6] It is also gradually reintegrating the working class into their unions.

There is nothing like having an army of community activists to support unions in dispute. For nearly forty years we have been under attack from successive governments, but we are street fighters and there are more ways than one to skin a fat cat. Our community work has provided our industrial members with huge support in their struggles with employers, including on picket lines, with petitions, in building links and coalitions with other community organisations, and with social media, recruitment and organising.

For example, community members turned up at the Grangemouth oil refinery in Falkirk in 2013 to support industrial action against Jim Ratcliff's relentless anti-union campaign, a struggle so vividly described in the book by Unite activist Mark Lyon.[7] In London, members protested against Crossrail over its blacklisting of trade unionists. Others campaigned against RBS bank branch closures, while members in Leicester supported an industrial campaign at the DPD depot in Hinckley. Community members have also thrown themselves into organising work, including recruitment and organising campaigns in hospitals, and demonstrations outside Premier Inn hotels to highlight poor working conditions at the hotel chain.

The Sports Direct campaign in 2016 would not have had nearly the impact it did without the collaboration of our Community members. Through their activism in thirty cities we were able to expose the retailer's shameful and abusive work practices and culture of fear, collecting 20,000 signatures on a petition, ultimately forcing it to scrap its zero-hour contracts, a move soon followed by Wetherspoons. This demonstrated how a strong and clear trade union response can protect workers and call out bad bosses, while engaging with thousands of people in the community not in paid employment. It also demonstrated that trade unions can and do reach out to low-paid gig economy workers, with all the challenges that presents. Trade unions organising in communities may well be one of the keys to changing today's economy and world of work in dramatic ways.

There are no rules about how to build a fairer society, which is why the role Community members play in our industrial disputes and campaigns has had such an impact, passing on the value of trade union membership through word of mouth and their work on the ground.

The GMB's fight for recognition at Amazon has focused on mobilising the communities within a thirty-five-mile radius of its warehouses, which were 'offering jobs of last resort'. The strategy, as it was told to me, was to 'make ourselves annoying wasps' outside Amazon sites, while talking directly to workers by a number of means. Most Amazon warehouses in the UK are in hard-to-get-to locations, so a good majority of the workers use special bus services, which they have to pay for. This makes it difficult for unions to make contact with them. But the GMB has managed to get its people onto those buses to talk directly to workers, much to the fury of the company. The union has also used village halls, church halls and community centres to host its own 'pop-up' community hubs in locations near Amazon depots, providing focal points not just for Amazon employees but for other workers in insecure jobs too. The union has, in effect, been 'organis-ing' communities as if they were themselves workplaces.

And what a day they had on Black Friday 2018, demon-strating outside Amazon depots, demanding that the firm stop treating its workers like robots.[8]

Enabling people to come together is one of the essential ingredients of trade unionism. Ever since I was a young shop steward, and all my life as a trade unionist, I have consistently learned that by working together we are able to challenge power and wealth, whether in a company, in the community or in the political arena.

I have met many Unite Community members who felt they had nowhere to go for help and advice, that they needed to find an outlet for their anger and do something about the injustices they and others in their communi-ties had experienced. They need their voice to be heard and they say that being part of the union makes them feel proud and gives them a sense of belonging. It also adds up to so much more than just being part of individual small campaigns. 'It's better to do things together, rather than struggle alone', one member said.

When you're not in work and you're sitting there alone and getting really angry about the unfairness of the benefits regime or whatever, you can go along to your branch meeting and try to do something about it, even if it's just holding protests and trying to spread awareness. Of course we won't always win, but we'll know that we've tried. And we make friends that way.

Local campaigns have included food bank collections, protesting against cuts to school breakfast clubs, fighting to save school transport for children with special needs, resisting the back-door privatisation of NHS trusts, and challenging the unfair treatment of asylum seekers.

This commitment to helping some of the most vulnerable people in society is fundamental to the incredible work that our voluntary sector members are doing day in day out. Unite represents over 60,000 workers in the community, youth and not-for-profit sectors, in a very diverse range of organisations, including charities, advice and legal bodies, youth and play schemes, housing associations and faith groups.

I was particularly proud when we opened the doors of our central London headquarters to homeless Londoners as an emergency shelter during one of the coldest of winter snaps, working with our members at the St Mungo's charity and the mayor of London.

I set out in Chapter 3 the importance of trade union education in giving working people a voice. I've visited many workplaces where we have opened up union learning centres through the Union Learning Fund (ULF), a government scheme which enables workers to learn at work, and from which employers benefit hugely (hence it hasn't, as yet, been scrapped, even by the Tories). I've spoken to older men and women who have effectively dodged their way through life without an education, unable to read and write, but who, directly through their union, have become confident in literacy and numeracy. Some unions have also set up community learning centres with ULF money, providing opportunities for family and friends of trade unionists to drop in and learn new skills, particularly in IT. I'm told that one of the most popular ULF courses has been Spanish, which employees have learned for fun.

I am passionate in my belief that learning should include teaching school children about the role of trade unions in communities and the wider society. Unions feature little on secondary school curricula, despite the fact that we are the largest voluntary organisations in the country. This is not surprising, of course, given what successive education secretaries have done to the national curriculum, but it is little wonder that young people enter the world of work knowing next to nothing about what trade unions do.

Alex Usher has not joined a union yet because she's still at school. She, probably alone among her schoolmates, understands what unions are because her parents are trade unionists. This is what she says: 'I think it's important for unions to find ways to show young people why our rights at work are important, why unions are relevant to us and why we should join one on our first day at work. Give us history lessons – show us how it was for people working fifty years ago and make it mean something to us now.'

And we must.

Back in 1914, pupils at the Burston school in Norfolk demonstrated that they knew a thing or two about unions and about solidarity. That year they embarked on the longest strike in history in defence of two principled, socialist teachers, sacked by their bosses for their beliefs and activities, including their support for the agricultural workers' union, which was recruiting at the time. The Burston strike stood for good, equal education for working-class kids; it demonstrates the timelessness of the struggles we still have to win, and shows how vital it is that we hang on to what is rightfully ours. When I spoke at the Burston rally a few years ago I talked about how the historic strike school building stands as a living monument to rural democracy and working-class education, and how we can learn from the strength and courage of the school children and the parents and community that supported them.

When I was a teenager, living in a trade union city, I knew about the unions. But when I go back to Liverpool now, young people struggle to explain what a union is. Go to many other cities and they really do not have a clue. That's why I took the view that, if no one else was teaching our children about trade unions, then the unions needed to do it themselves, by visiting every school to tell every fifteen- and sixteen-year-old what trade unionism is.

When we set up our 'Unite in Schools' initiative the *Sun* newspaper attacked us for trying to recruit kids. But our schools programme is not about promoting Unite or recruiting school pupils. We simply explain what unions are and facilitate debate about the role they play and about the rights and responsibilities we all have. This is important because these young people, about to go out to work for the first time, may well be exploited and will need to understand the concept of collectivism if they are to do anything about that. The Unite in Schools project has demonstrated that school students can become passionate advocates for collective strength. Of course, some schools have been resistant, but many have embraced the programme.

6

PLAYING OUR PART IN POLITICS

They have the money, we have the people.

Bernie Sanders

Everything we do as citizens is determined by politics; and therefore everything unions do is determined by politics. There is an organic connection between the different parts of working-class lives: in the community, at work and in politics. This is a principle that goes back to the foundation of the Labour Party.

As previously noted, the outcome of the 1900 Taff Vale railway strike led the unions to conclude that they needed a voice in Parliament. A decade before Taff Vale, the Leeds gasworkers' strike of 1890 had also woken its leaders to the hollow stance of many supposedly radical organisations, particularly the Liberal Party. Tom Maguire was one of the leaders of that strike and of the new unionism movement in the city. He had been advocating the establishment of a Socialist Labour Party for some time. After the gasworkers' strike – which also saw walkouts in Bristol, London and elsewhere – exposed the extent to which the Liberals were not on the side of working people, Maguire's ideas, and those of his comrades such as Tom Mann and Will Thorne, started to gain traction. Like Taff Vale, the gasworkers' strike was an important chapter in the founding of the Independent Labour Party, which went on to play a key role in the formation of the Labour Representation Committee (LRC), the direct predecessor to today's Labour Party.

The LRC was formed in the same year as the Taff Vale strike, following a motion passed at the Trades Union Congress annual conference that instructed the TUC to bring together left-wing organisations and form them into a single body that would sponsor parliamentary candidates. This was done at a special conference attended by trade unionists and others, and two of the LRC's candidates, including the future Labour Party leader Keir Hardie, were successful in winning a seat in Parliament at the general election of that year, in spite of the short time there was to campaign.

Almost immediately, union affiliation to the LRC rose dramatically. This period also saw the tabling of the Trade Dispute Act. In the 1906 election, the LRC returned twenty-nine MPs to Parliament, and at their first meeting they formally adopted the name the Labour Party. Keir Hardie became the party's chairman, and swiftly moved to get the Trade Disputes Act passed.

The founding of the Labour Party demonstrates how trade unions, and trade unionists, do not live in isolation. We are part of a community, of society, working and fighting side by side. And we have a fundamental, historic and central role within British politics.

I recall Thatcher's infamous declaration that there is 'no such thing as society'. There is. There is such a thing as community, community spirit, people helping each other. There is collectivism everywhere. Victoria Egerton, a young union rep in Manchester, told me that when trying to recruit young people she doesn't just focus on convincing them of the importance of unity, winning better pay and providing support for people in difficulties at work. The opportunity to campaign on wider political issues is an attraction of trade unionism too:

> Social justice campaigns are important for young people. But being a trade unionist is not about single issue campaigning – join Greenpeace if that's what you want. Trade unions campaign on so many issues – currently, among other things, the living wage, period dignity and to stop Universal Credit – and we also encourage members to run their own actions.
>
> Getting involved with the union's political strategies can be particularly exciting and rewarding. For example, our young members' committees have been working hard to get the support of MPs for a Bill that will extend

the National Living Wage to young workers. It's not just petition signing with unions, it's getting directly involved in lobbying MPs and working industrially in our workplaces to try to build support and influence for something that will make a huge difference to our lives.

This is the essence of trade unionism, and why it is vitally important that we engage in politics and political campaigns that may not appear to be directly related to saving jobs or increasing wages. It is why tens of thousands of trade unionists who do not work in the NHS, as well as those who do, have been out on the streets in the last few years, and particularly in 2018, the seventieth anniversary of the creation of our health service, defending it from the privatisation vultures, demanding it be restored to its users. It is also why, in February 2003, the biggest march we have ever seen on our streets was full of trade unionists saying of the coming war in Iraq: 'Not in my name.'

Trade unions have been central to progressive political campaigns since their foundation and have played a central role in the anti-war movement, though it took time to bring them all on board, as Andrew Murray and Lindsey German explain in their story of the Stop the War movement.[1] It was the smaller unions with left-wing leaderships at the time, including RMT, ASLEF, the FBU and NATFHE that led the way in supporting the Stop the War Coalition from its formation in 2001 shortly after the attacks on New York's twin towers.

Although most of the bigger unions, including my own, passed strong policies on peace and internationalism at their national conferences, there was, as Murray and German point out, a reluctance to fall out with New Labour over its pro-war stance. But by the September 2002 Labour Party conference most affiliated unions opposed the government's position, and it was only the support of the constituency Labour parties that carried the leadership's line.

Nevertheless, while the unions exerted what influence they could over the Blair administration, Thatcher's anti-union laws still prevented them from taking direct action, including industrial action, in support of their anti-war position. Even so, the unilateral action taken by two train drivers in Scotland – both ASLEF members – in refusing to move trains loaded with armaments bound for the Gulf, and whose employer did not take action against them or their union, very much puts me in mind of those determined Rolls-Royce workers who refused to work on the Chilean air force's Hawker Hunters. My earlier point stands: no union is incapable of getting around the laws intended to shackle us.

In the 1960s, I got involved in protests against the Vietnam War, which had suddenly come into our living rooms through television. I campaigned too against apartheid in South Africa, a struggle that trade unions were at the forefront of, as they were in the civil rights movement in America. And I was deeply active against the 1973 right-wing coup in Chile, in which thousands of trade unionists were murdered by General Pinochet's henchmen. I worked on the ships in the Port of Liverpool that serviced Chile's imports and exports, and I heard the stories from Chilean crew members.

Why get involved in such international struggles as a British trade unionist? Because these were deep injustices perpetrated against working people, just as those committed against working people and trade unionists in Britain were, including the Shrewsbury 24, the Pentonville Five, the striking miners at Orgreave, the Tolpuddle Martyrs and those killed and injured at the Peterloo Massacre. What was done to them, by the state, was quite simply criminal.

Look too at the Palestinian cause. Here, the majority of British trade unions are affiliated to the Palestine Solidarity Campaign. All are committed by policy decisions taken through their democratic structures – ultimately their national conference – to demand justice for the Palestinians. Just as with apartheid in South Africa, international solidarity can make a key contribution in any liberation struggle, and over the last decade there has been a surge in trade union solidarity action with the people of Palestine.

Being trade unionists enables us to immerse ourselves in struggles for peace and justice across the world. It is also possible to focus on particular areas, such as exposing and targeting firms complicit in the arms trade, while building campaigns within unions at both local and national levels.

People ask me how such campaigns impact on trade union members. My response is that they impact on the world in which we live in, a world that has changed, that is no longer a distant place. Internationalism is the very essence of trade unionism and it has always been with me. We have to develop international links of solidarity, and I've worked with many international unions in doing so.

And before I hear cries of protest about union members' subs being used for political campaigning rather than winning better pay and conditions, any trade union wanting to spend money on party political activities is bound by law to set up a separate political fund.[2] No member is obliged to contribute and, since 2016, new members are required to actively opt-in to contribute. This was a deliberate move by the government intended to reduce our political spending power, which should tell us just how important our role in politics is.

When I became a T&G regional officer, on top of my industrial duties I also became the North West's political officer. The union had not had one before, and my job was to coordinate the union's input into constituency Labour parties (CLPs), including organising delegates to them. That experience formed the basis of my idea, many years later as general secretary, that Unite needed a proper political strategy.

I have never seen or believed in, as part of the struggle for fairness and justice for working people, a difference between the industrial and the political fight. It was always clear to me that if the right kind of government was in power there would be a greater chance of that justice and of a fair deal. I have been consistent in my view that only a socialist government, committed to trade union rights, can give us that. This has inevitably meant battling within the Labour Party for the best policies and leadership, and is why I always disagreed with the modernisers and their embracing of neoliberalism, as much as I was delighted when Labour came to power in 1997.

So I make no apology for the role Unite played as a trade union in 2017, in bringing a radical progressive Labour Party to the threshold of power, when most others doubted this was possible. Whenever the mainstream media and Tory MPs attack the unions for funding the Labour Party, they, deliberately in my opinion, overlook the fact that the party has always been the political arm of our movement. While partisan politics will never get in the way of fighting for industries, jobs, communities and investment, the trade union link with Labour remains fundamental to what we are as a movement.

Trade unions have been moving to the left pretty much since Margaret Thatcher kicked them out of their economic role in British capitalism, and New Labour did not restore it. This freed them up to work in different ways, rather than just backing whoever was most likely to win a Labour leadership election, which is how things tended to happen in the past. The emergence of the so-called awkward squad of union leaders in the early 2000s represented not just a political, but a generational shift in trade union politics.[3] They did not all survive in the leadership of their unions, but they were without a doubt a weather vane for the political direction the unions were going in.

Alex Nunns, in his book *The Candidate*,[4] which charts Jeremy Corbyn's path to power, describes how at the Tolpuddle Martyrs festival in 2015, in the middle of the Labour leadership campaign, Corbyn told the crowd: 'We can win people back but we don't do it by apologising for what we are . . . We do it by being proud of what we are, proud of where we come from, proud of our unions.' His leadership election victory was a tribute to all seven trade unions that nominated and campaigned for him. Unite members took part in the leadership election in their thousands, enthused by the chance to engage in a genuine debate about what and who Labour stands for, and the sort of nation we want modern Britain to be.

Second time around, during the attempted coup in 2016, when right-wing Labour MPs forced another leadership election and tried to prevent Jeremy Corbyn's name being on the ballot paper, it was Unite that made sure it was. We had lawyers working for Corbyn when the Labour Party's own lawyers were insisting the rules required him to get fifty nominations and that being the incumbent didn't allow him to go forward automatically. Our assistant general secretary for legal services, Howard Beckett, went in fighting. And we succeeded.

This did not make us popular with everyone. There will always be those who persist in challenging trade unions when they get involved in party politics, claiming we do not represent our members when we do. I am unlikely to forget the accusations, when I was standing for re-election as Unite general secretary in 2017, that I spend too much time on Westminster politics and should focus instead on representing my members. I still scratch my head at that. So much of what Unite has secured for its members, what the labour movement has won for working people, has been achieved through our involvement in politics – at Westminster, in the devolved parliaments and locally.

But I am nonetheless extremely conscious that many of our members do not vote Labour. And that's why I supported the changes Labour made to its trade union affiliation rules in 2014 following the Collins Review, which brought about the new category of registered supporters of the party.[5] Many believed Collins, with its breaking of the electoral college, would water down the influence of trade unions in the Labour Party. And being the only trade union leader to support it was quite a difficult and lonely place to be for a while.

I remember how the colour drained from a BBC political correspondent's face when they interviewed me, expecting me to provide some explosive headlines with a furious attack on the Miliband–Collins proposals, but getting something rather tame instead. That was because I never saw it as a weakening of the union link, but rather as a step forward for our movement. It was an opportunity for the tens of thousands who had left the Labour Party during the New Labour era to come back to their political home, and for thousands more to join for the first time. And that is exactly what happened, reducing the huge influence of the most right-wing Parliamentary Labour Party (PLP) in living memory. Without that rule change, Jeremy Corbyn would never have become Labour leader. While I would like to be able to say that I foresaw the coming of Jeremy Corbyn – one of my famous predictions for which I am forever in trouble – I didn't.

Unite's political strategy is intended to get all members involved to play their part; in the first few weeks of the 2016 leadership contest 100,000 of our members became affiliate Labour Party supporters, as part of our union's democratic process, based on aims agreed by its executive council. When Jeremy Corbyn made it onto the ballot paper for the leadership contest, our executive council overwhelmingly backed him. This is exactly what our union's political strategy commits us to doing – winning working people for Labour by encouraging our members to get involved at all levels of the Labour Party, so it's truly representative of our society.

Trade unions are essential to society's wider democracy, and being a trade unionist gives working people a voice on the policy issues that are most important to them, their families and their communities. It gives them the opportunity to get involved in building broad alliances, working with other like-minded groups who support our values to fight back against cuts and austerity, and, most importantly, winning a Labour government that will govern in the interests of working people. I believe it's the duty of trade unions to ensure Labour finds a way back to power.

Because politics, radical politics, isn't going back in the box. Britain is crying out for an alternative to austerity economics and neoliberal dogma. And as trade unionists we need to fight for that.

The rights that British workers have today were gained over many decades, often reflecting more than two centuries of collective and political action by workers and their unions. My dad worked most of his life in ship repair, and was a member of a union that eventually became part of the construction union UCATT. I was presented with a wonderful framed poster of his union's banner at a Unite Scottish region event in Grangemouth, and it sits proudly on my office wall. There was no sick pay for my dad's generation then, but in his latter working years he got a maintenance job in a school, taking great pride in keeping it well painted; he was amazed that he was entitled to sick pay, but still he never took it, telling me that it was important the unions had won him the right to it, but that it should never be abused. My dad was the loveliest man I ever met and I was always guided by him; his words really impacted on me in terms of my approach to negotiating sick pay with employers. I always made it clear, and ensured shop stewards did the same, that we weren't asking for a perk that our members could exploit, but for a fundamentally fair working condition.

And this is how change happens. Back in 1987, at the T&G biennial delegate conference, a young woman delegate changed history. She moved a motion on the introduction of a statutory minimum wage, a brave and not altogether popular move because the left of the T&G had always opposed the minimum wage, believing it would stop free collective bargaining.

Yet that delegate, and another young woman who seconded it, in the face of executive committee opposition and a split in the left of the union, won the day, and campaigning for the minimum wage became union policy. A couple of months later it was incorporated into existing TUC and Labour Party policy, which led directly to it being adopted in the 1992 Labour manifesto, before being introduced by the Labour government in 1997.

If we're looking for evidence of the importance of being a trade unionist and of how it can impact on real lives, then there it is. But the power of lobbying – actions taken to influence government decision-making and policy – is also empowering. Our members at the Bombardier Aviation facility in Belfast – which makes the wings for its C-series passenger jets and whose whole future was threatened by US protectionism – will attest to that. In 2017, we had decisions taken by one multinational company in the US against another in Canada, which were going to have a devastating effect on the Northern Ireland economy. We raised the issue with Bombardier, and they agreed with us, but there was nothing the management in Belfast could do.

So the unions engaged in the political arena and mobilised workers in their thousands. They walked the halls of Westminster seeking the support of politicians, and gave evidence before parliamentary committees to raise awareness. The transatlantic campaign took them to Montreal and Washington to make the case to the Canadian and US administrations and find common cause with sister unions, while every council in Northern Ireland was spoken to. All this work was to try to persuade them to demand that Boeing take a different stance, or at least to try to influence the outcome of the US department of commerce ruling.

As our ministers in Westminster weakly pleaded with Donald Trump in their attempts to press Washington into a U-turn, and just as his commerce department was preparing to slap tariffs of 300 per cent on Bombardier's jets, we were working politically to save skilled jobs in Belfast. In the absence of any clear effort by politicians or the UK government, who appeared to wave the white flag over Whitehall in the fight to save jobs, skills and communities in Belfast and across Northern Ireland, and in the midst of a corporate dispute raging above their heads, it was workers, trade unionists, who took the fight on.

I cannot imagine what the campaign to save Bombardier jobs would have looked like, much less what it would have achieved, without such a high-profile, and intense, political campaign.

Steel provides another great example of trade union political work. In 2015 we fought to save what was left of our steel industry, when Unite, steel union Community and the GMB took the Save our Steel campaign out of their workplaces and onto the streets, forcing a Tory government to step in and protect the industry from the threat of cheap Chinese imports. The threat to the future of our national asset, part of an industry adding £95 billion to our national wealth, bringing in £12 billion in taxes and providing good, well-paid jobs, was a political issue and we needed a political campaign to respond to it.

Cameron's government was prepared to let our steel manufacturing go down the pan because it believed the market was king. But I met with the then business secretary Sajid Javid several times and, incredibly for a government that worshipped at the altar of the market and non-intervention, he agreed to take a 25 per cent stake in the industry should it be needed. Fast forward to 2019, when British Steel's shady private financiers Greybull, who bought the company for £1 in 2015, were about to walk away, leaving the steelmaker to fall into insolvency. It was our lobbying work, with the then business secretary Greg Clark in particular, that put the company into official receivership underwritten by government, enabling it to continue trading as a going concern until a buyer could be found.

Politically then, the role of trade unions is central. We will always fight for our members regardless of the party in government. The Bombardier campaign demonstrates

exactly why unions have to be political, why they have to
fight both politically and industrially. And that includes
entering into dialogue with Tory ministers when our
members' needs and jobs demand it.

But how do we decide on what policies to stand for? The
mainstream media like to portray the image of trade union
barons waking up in the morning and suddenly deciding
on a policy issue. It is not like that. Unions are democratic
organisations and our lay member activists determine both
our industrial and political direction. Unite's shop stewards are the critical springboard for campaigns, which
often require political action.

When I was a young shop steward we campaigned for all
ancillary workers to be registered, just as the dockers were.
It was a desperately important issue for me and my family
and for thousands of ancillary workers. Registration meant
job security and an end to the casualisation of our work.
We launched a massive political campaign, and I was part
of the delegation that met with the Labour government's
employment secretary, Michael Foot. And yet the legislation to make it happen was defeated in Parliament because
three Labour MPs voted against their government. Which
is why I say that while Labour has always stood for fairness, justice, peace and strong communities, it has not
always practised this. New Labour certainly did not fulfil
that commitment in government. But I absolutely believe
that Labour remains the party of hope, ready to take on

any government hell-bent on making life worse for ordinary people.

There have always been both left-wing and right-wing unions, and I am glad I joined a left-wing one from the start. Unite, like the T&G before it, has always taken the view that we need to win back the values that were beginning to be lost: solidarity, community spirit, fighting back and challenging the establishment – which was, after all, the very reason the Labour Party was founded.

This is why it is so important to try to get people into Parliament who reflect those views, who understand our members' experiences. I am sometimes misquoted as saying we need more working-class MPs, but I have never actually said that. What I have always said is we need more MPs who reflect our values. After all, my great political hero, Tony Benn, who inspired me to join the Labour Party in 1970, could hardly be described as working class. In contrast, I have known many MPs from working-class backgrounds who have been deeply right-wing and opposed to our values. I recognise that lots of working-class people vote Conservative, so it's no real mystery that there are Labour MPs not committed to taking on the establishment.

We've been very lucky in Unite in recent times to be able to promote some great young people as parliamentary candidates – real fighters, feisty people who are proud to be trade unionists and to fight for our values. The MPs Dan Carden, Laura Pidcock, Marsha de Cordova and

Rebecca Long-Bailey all went through our future candidates programme,[6] which aims to build confidence and skills among Labour activists who want to become party candidates, and we've helped others, including Angela Rayner. And now there's a new generation of young leaders beginning to emerge in our union who will follow them and, I believe, become great politicians. That's an opportunity that surely merits being a trade unionist.

7
FIGHTING FOR EQUALITY

A woman's place is in her union.

Anonymous

For me, trade unionism is about collectivism. And class. It's about all working people, fighting together for fairness and justice, opposing all forms of discrimination and exploitation. Unions, and the wider labour movement, have changed people's lives. They are a force for equality that all workers should be a part of.

Income inequality has grown since the 1970s. The changes the Tories made to collective bargaining in the 1980s made it much more difficult to organise workers on a sectoral basis, and while living standards had previously taken great strides forward, after Thatcher became prime minister they slipped steadily back, in parallel with the decline in the ability of trade unions to collectively negotiate pay and conditions for members.

However, for trade unions, equality cannot be about pay alone. It has to have a special focus on those workers who are always disadvantaged. Which is why a core Unite objective, written into our rulebook, is to promote equality and fairness for all, including equality structures with full constitutional status for women, BAEM, disabled and LGBT members. It also demands that we actively oppose prejudice and discrimination on grounds of gender, race, ethnic origin, religion, class, marital status, sexual orientation, gender identity, age, disability or caring responsibilities. Of course rulebooks cannot achieve such objectives in themselves, but they do set trade unions and trade unionists clear paths for positive action that can make a difference.

In reading that rule again I am proud that it includes class as one of the characteristics for which we protect our members from being treated with disrespect and unfairness. I know that class is not a much used or understood concept these days, and the media would have it that we live in a classless society, save perhaps for the aristocracy at the top of the pile. But we cannot ignore the fact that top chief executives earn 133 times more than the average worker,[1] or that we live in the fifth richest yet one of the most unequal countries in the developed world. With these statistics, it is impossible to claim that class divisions have disappeared.

~

The Equal Pay Act, as well as landmark legal cases such as *Pickstone v Freemans*[2] (a trade-union-backed work for equal value case) and *Enderby v Frenchay Health Authority*[3] (a group equal pay case involving hundreds of speech therapists who were members of one of Unite's predecessor unions, MSF), have been hard fought for and have undoubtedly advanced equality. But how as trade unionists do we deal with institutional inequality issues that a legal case might expose but not necessarily end? For example, exposing workplace harassment in the hospitality sector. Unions have been campaigning on harassment and giving a voice to victims for years, and I salute the courage of everyone who has spoken out about the abuse they have suffered.

During the phenomenal growth of the #MeToo campaign, which shone a light on power and its abuse within multiple industries, the hospitality sector of our union carried out a survey of its members. Called #NotOnTheMenu, its results were a damning indictment of an industry in which harassment is endemic. Nearly all respondents had experienced sexual harassment first-hand, most had received unwelcome and inappropriate touching and kissing, and the percentage that had received requests for sexual favours was shocking.

Trade unions have a duty to uncover the extent of such issues, but also to work with members and employers to find solutions. This means negotiating dignity at work policies: real, effective policies with clear sets of values and a zero-tolerance approach to inappropriate behaviour. We also need to understand what is propelling the rise of unstable work environments, in which no one can find a human resources department, or a manager able to deal with reports of sexual harassment or any other grievance. Often in such places there is no union rep or collective voice to call out the abuses, because we can't get in there. Without that support, workers will continue to lack the confidence to complain about inequality, discrimination and harassment, and will continue to fear losing their jobs if they do.

Discrimination divides working people, and it can divide us too as trade unionists unless we take action within our movement to prevent it. I am a big supporter of trade union equality reps, and believe that they can make important progress and drive forward change. This is why as a union we try to ensure that all our workplaces and branches have equality reps, why we have union equality education courses, and why, in the political arena, we have been fighting so hard for equality reps to have statutory rights – the same rights that health and safety reps have, which have already had such an impact on workers' lives. As well as saving tens of thousands of lives, those rights have changed the culture. Suddenly, employers started talking about health and safety being their number one priority. This was hugely significant, but let there be no mistake, it was trade unions that achieved it. Likewise, inequality is something we can and must change.

I am convinced that union equality reps can have the same massive impact, and that securing statutory rights for them will be a huge breakthrough when it comes to equality at work. Without those rights, unions depend on being able to reach agreement with individual employers to recognise equality reps. Some do, but many do not.

The unfair treatment of any group of workers impacts on all working people. Real equality at work will transform the prospects of all workers, all communities, and in all areas of the economy. Strong trade unions can deliver that, if they are enabled to do so by progressive governments.

I was involved in the political campaigning that eventually brought about the Equal Pay Act of 1970, entitling women to the same pay and conditions as men. But it has been women who have led the fight for their rights at work, for equal pay and treatment, and who have achieved many landmark victories, often in the teeth of opposition from government, employers and even from some in their own unions.

I think of my own experiences growing up in Liverpool, seeing my mother fight for her rights and how she had to give up her job in Blackledges bakery when she married my dad because they, like many firms, did not employ married women. Later she worked in an old-style family clothes shop where she did eventually gain seniority, becoming responsible for buying from the warehouses, the only woman among men choosing the stock – her way of breaking the glass ceiling. She was always encouraging and proud of the women in our family fighting for their equal rights.

Through my trade union education, I learned about the courageous and strong women throughout history who sacrificed and won so much for equality and against discrimination. And of course I have known and worked with many inspirational trade union women who have continued those earlier struggles, often struggling for support within the union too. That's why, when I was a national officer, I made sure that equality was always on the agenda, and we talked about action for equality, rather than merely paying it lip service. The challenge to act and not just talk – coming from trade union sisters such as Sally Keegan and Brenda Sanders, who are sadly no longer with us, and many others – changed our union for the better.

I hardly know where to start in paying tribute to those working women of all ages and circumstances, working all types of shifts, in all sorts of industries and sectors, on the land, in factories for the war effort, exploited in their homes, fighting for a right to be paid the same as their male counterparts, or even to receive a living wage. These are women who have achieved so much for their class, making advances not just for themselves but for all women, all workers and for all people who have faced, and continue to face, inequality and discrimination at work and within our wider society.

The 1889 London match girls strike, as mentioned, was a key moment in early British trade union history. Then there were the women chain makers of Cradley Heath, members of the National Federation of Women Workers (NFWW), working in 'sweated' labour conditions from their homes, paid piece rates according to the weight and quantity of the chain.[4] Led by Mary Macarthur, the Scottish trade unionist and peace campaigner, the workers went on strike in 1910, demanding to be paid the agreed minimum wage for the industry. Their victory had a huge impact across the labour movement. NFWW membership soared, while awareness of the issues of low pay and non-payment of minimum rates increased.

The film *Made in Dagenham* was hugely entertaining, but it told the story of real women who understood why they should be trade unionists, and how solidarity in the face of not only a hostile employer, but also a reluctant union leadership, could leverage change. In 1968, the 187 women machinists at the Ford car factory in East London, members of the T&G, walked off the shop floor when their jobs were downgraded, resulting in a significant pay cut, while men doing similar jobs stayed on their grade.

The walkout, which lasted four weeks, halted car production. It ended after an intervention by Barbara Castle, who offered the women 92 per cent of what the men were paid. The strike paved the way for the Equal Pay Act, though it took until 1984, and another six-week strike, before the women machinists actually received equal pay.

It's important to acknowledge that the Dagenham women had to battle not only against the bosses, but also against the male-dominated bureaucracy within their union. This reflects my experience, from being involved in the liberation movement for women, that prejudices within our unions can be as big an obstacle as employers are. Of course it was common in those days for women to be paid less than their male colleagues, but today women still get paid on average a fifth less than men, which is why trade unions are still fighting for equal pay for all workers.

It amused me when a review in the *Daily Telegraph* of the subsequent stage version of *Made in Dagenham* described the movie as 'one of the most loved British films of recent years'.[5] How quaint, for such a virulently anti-union paper.

And onto Grunwick, the film-processing plant in north London where mainly Asian women struck for over forty weeks in 1976, demanding equal pay and union recognition.[6] I received my first experience of 'kettling' (police confinement of demonstrators in a very small area) on that picket line. I had travelled down to London in the early hours with my shop steward mates. We were sitting by the side of the road and word came that the scabs were about to be brought in, so we got up to stop them and were blocked by the police. I was enormously in admiration of all the women who led that strike.

Then there were the Sky Chef workers, again mainly Asian women, who were sacked in the late 1990s by Lufthansa for daring to go on strike against the imposition of new contracts and working practices, and their replacement with agency workers.[7] Later came the Gate Gourmet strikers, most of them women, whose jobs preparing in-flight meals for BA customers were contracted out.[8] The company started replacing them with agency workers on lower pay, then sacked over 700 of the workforce for refusing to return to work on that pay scale and with vastly reduced terms and conditions – Gate Gourmet's plan all along.

In the mid-1990s, there was also the Hillingdon Hospital dispute, a three-year-long strike led by low-paid, women cleaners, sacked for refusing to accept disgraceful cuts in pay and conditions after the hospital awarded the support services contract to Pall Mall Services Group. I was proud to share platforms with the women of Hillingdon Hospital.

The docks in my time were almost exclusively male, and white. I rarely saw a woman at work, or a black worker. The dockers had a policy that jobs that came up went to their sons. I don't justify that, but I understand that they saw it as defending good jobs for their families and the community against bad bosses and scab labour. They had suffered tremendous hardship as a result of the bosses dividing workers and using scabs to break strikes. They had fought hard for their gains and by 'keeping it in the family' solidarity was guaranteed.

The Bristol Bus Boycott of 1963 arose from the refusal of the Bristol Omnibus Company to employ black or

Asian bus crews. Fifty years later, Unite apologised for the T&G's support of the management's racist policy.[9] The Unite education booklet about Mohammad Taj – the TUC's first Muslim president – tells of the part he played in taking on racism in the bus industry and within the union in Bradford.[10] It is another example of our movement's own chequered past on discrimination.

When I became a T&G officer, dealing with many industries and a huge number of women workers, I quickly saw the reality of discrimination in our workplaces, and that the Equal Pay Act wasn't having the impact it was supposed to. There were so many jobs – more or less exclusively women's jobs – that were being paid significantly less than those that were predominantly male. And men were receiving bonuses even if the basic pay of men and women was the same.

During that time I worked with many tough, fighting women. Those working in food factories were the backbone of the T&G. And then there were the contract cleaners, campaigning for a living wage. As a young regional officer, walking into those meetings of mainly women shop stewards was a little daunting at first, but I remember well the charm, warmth and friendliness of those sisters.

There have been many breakthroughs, though few of them easy. In fighting for equality we have had to bring all our members with us, especially white men, arguing for what is right and winning round members and employers alike to those arguments. That means standing up to any attempt by employers to divide us by, for example, cutting men's pay or women's hours in answer to our demands for an end to unfair treatment.

I've worked to drive equality onto the negotiating agenda. In wage negotiations, we typically go in with, say, ten demands and before long about five of them have fallen off the agenda. Invariably, in the past, it was always the equality issues that were dropped, and it was this that I wanted to address. For academics and lawyers, these might appear to be easy issues, but when you're involved in difficult negotiations and the employer isn't budging, it's not easy to keep equality issues centre stage. Which again is why I have so much faith and hope in the ability of union equality reps, with statutory rights, to make a real difference.

Of course there is a way to go yet in achieving greater equality in our members' workplaces, as well as within the unions' own structures. Our union must be representative of the workforce it represents in order to strengthen organisation and build our membership. We have a strong commitment to 'equality at the heart of our union', but this must be a call to action not just a commitment in words. That is why we are also committed to ensuring a minimum 'proportionality' in the representation of women and black and Asian ethnic minorities throughout our structures, and to positive action for disabled and LGBT+ membership as well. The words 'minimum proportionality' might sound bureaucratic, but it was working-class women in our union who led the drive for this policy, and what it has achieved in practice has been incredible.

I remember well when women and black members were barely represented at our union conferences. Times have changed, but I do recognise that terms like proportionality do not mean an awful lot to female members on a factory floor or in an office who aren't getting the same pay as their male colleagues. That is why we need to turn such phrases and policies into real-life action against continuing inequalities.

So while the majority of trade union members are women, and the number of women in Unite is bigger than in many individual unions, some unions, including Unite, still have a predominantly male membership. This is reflected in our officers too, although the picture is changing and we can be rightly proud of the progress we've made, while never being complacent about what is needed. Only in the last seven years have we had our first woman TUC general secretary, Frances O'Grady.

But how do we encourage more women, black, disabled and LGBT+ workers to be active at grassroots level, as shop stewards and branch officers? This is a challenge not just for Unite, but for the whole labour movement. And again, it is a commitment that our equality sectors are prioritising, encouraging their members to stand for election to workplace rep and branch officer positions, to make sure they have a voice in the union that they can take into the workplace too. But, in doing that, they are also working at making it easier to get involved in the union, with equality education courses and action to tackle potential barriers such as the time and venue of meetings, childcare, caring and disability access.

None of this is about tokenism. It is about education and encouragement, ensuring that the trade unionists who lead the fight for true equality in our workplaces reflect the diversity of those workplaces and are capable and good at doing their job.

Another fight for jobs I was deeply involved with during my time as a union officer and assistant general secretary was at Remploy, the organisation set up in 1944 by Ernest Bevin, then minister of labour. Remploy was an important component of Clement Attlee's post-war welfare state programme, providing good jobs, real jobs, for disabled people. I was chair of the trade union consortium during the 1990s, involving seven other unions, with the GMB the largest, and brilliantly led on the consortium by Phil Davies. Remploy had workers in eighty-four factories scattered around the country, from Penzance to Aberdeen, making high-quality products.

But Bevin's eventual Tory successor, employment secretary Michael Portillo, wrecked it all. In 1994 he used the European Union as a bogeyman to claim that the government needed to impose competitive tendering for its own contracts. The argument was also made that more disabled people could be supported if government money was used differently. There was a strong disability-led lobby against Remploy – arguing that it was a form of segregating disabled workers – as well as the trade union campaign in support of it.

This created a very emotive situation. I did not accept the better use of money argument; it was an example of neoliberalism at its worst. The way the government was trying to close these factories was awful, affecting so many decent people who were desperate to continue to work and to contribute. One of the factories made uniforms for British Army soldiers going into desert-based conflict zones and at risk of chemical exposure. The contract was given instead to a company in Lithuania, and it was later revealed that their product didn't provide proper protection.

I met so many committed and powerful disabled trade unionists during that campaign. And while factory after factory closed, we managed to halt the closure programme for a while, with the help of the then deputy prime minister John Prescott, who intervened after we raised the Remploy fight at Labour's national executive committee. We undoubtedly saved some factories and kept others open a bit longer. But the harsh truth was that whenever a factory closed, a year later 80 per cent of its workforce had not found new work and were on benefits. The Tories started this disgraceful dismantling of skilled, specialist work for disabled people, who have faced the full force of austerity and cuts since, and the New Labour government only continued the wrecking process.

~

Austerity has had a similar impact more generally, creating insecure jobs and a transient workforce removed from traditional communities, bussed into anonymous warehouses servicing the retail sector. Workers are employed on zero-hour contracts, not knowing when the next bit of work will come, working so many different shift patterns that they rarely meet the same colleagues twice. And they are without the protection of trade union membership and collective bargaining. All these injustices fuel inequality.

We know, for example, that black, Asian and minority ethnic workers are more likely than white workers to be stuck in temporary, zero-hour work or other insecure jobs, with all the associated low pay rates and discriminatory working practices. And inevitably BAME women have been the worst affected. This is nothing short of racism in the labour market.

I have seen all kinds of discrimination against our black members over the decades, in many of the companies I've had dealings with, and I've always challenged it. I know it still exists, and we continue to fight for non-discriminatory pay in the industrial arena. But it sometimes feels like so much of the progress trade unions have made on equality is being lost in the new economy. This is why unions must work harder to organise in these sectors, in spite of the barriers.

Labour's 2017 manifesto recognised the need for an industrial strategy that will ensure long-term investment in our infrastructure and guarantee a fair deal for workers, including better wages and tackling insecure work. I am convinced that its commitment to a twenty-point plan for security and equality at work, including giving statutory rights for union equality reps and taking decisive action to end the exploitation of migrant labour by greedy bosses, will transform our prospects as a country, in all our economic sectors.

Unionised workplaces are not only safer, they are also more equal. This is why we need stronger unions, unions from which everyone can benefit, and why working women need to be in a union and to become trade unionists. Only strong trade unions, made strong by their members, can bargain and win better wages for all workers, achieve equal pay for work of equal value, and end prejudice against any group of people in the workplace.

8

CONCLUSION: RISE LIKE LIONS

Unions are a major inconvenience to those that want to exploit and steal from the working class.

Emily Blunt, actor

Ryanair's chief executive Michael O'Leary once said that hell would freeze over before he let trade unions through the company's door. The brand was synonymous with shoddy customer service and exploitative employment practices, to the extent that its cabin crew felt kicked from both sides – by bad bosses and angry customers.

Those crew desperately needed a trade union to give them a voice and I always hoped I'd see the day when they were organised and recognised and we'd be able to negotiate with the airline over pay, hours and holidays, and openly recruit without opposition from management. So what a victory for trade unionism it was when we achieved just that, signing a historic recognition agreement with Ryanair in 2018.

The agreement secured full consultation rights and collective bargaining for UK cabin crew and time off for their Unite reps to fulfil their union duties in representing members.

And hell still hasn't frozen over.

Being a trade unionist in Britain today means having to live and work with all the legal restrictions placed on us by a succession of Conservative governments. Trade unionism was further abused by the shameful refusal of the Labour governments of Blair and Brown to remove those constraints, during which time work became increasingly privatised and fragmented. With David Cameron's 2016 Trade Union Act, attempts were made to extend Thatcher's vision. It has all been designed to make life increasingly difficult for workers and trade unions.

There is no denying that the relentless attacks on trade unions in Britain have weakened us. This has led directly to a collective social amnesia in society in which generations of working people have no knowledge or memory of trade unions. Many young people, whose parents and grandparents have never been union members, and who do not read or watch mainstream media, cannot even offer the typically anti-union response we might expect from an older generation when approached to join. They simply do not know what we are.

Unless we reach young workers we cannot help them to understand or inform them. Our hospitality sector members have found that even before trying to recruit new members it first has to give them basic information, online and in leaflets, about what unions are, what they do and what they can achieve for working people. Unions need to sell the benefits of access to quality apprenticeships and skilled, well-paid, secure work, with pensions and promotion prospects. We need to persuade workers that joining a union will make them stronger. Above all, we need to make the next generation come to believe that there is something better than what they have now.

British unions have joined together in a powerful campaign led by the Communications Workers Union (CWU) called 'Winning a New Deal for Workers'. It is aimed at coordinating how unions respond to the organising challenges presented by the changing nature of work, protecting workers in precarious, casualised sectors, and winning basic rights to job security and a fair and living wage. How we do this is critical to our success, and 'relevance' is one of the most important words in trade unionism. What could be more relevant than the central role unions must have in relation to today's climate emergency?

Trade unions are needed in society to deal with issues beyond the workplace, including industrial strategy and investment questions. And these increasingly involve addressing the challenge of climate change, which is fundamentally a class and trade union issue. It is working-class people across the globe who suffer its devastating impacts, while the wealthy cash in.

Trade unions are driving forward Labour's vision of a green industrial revolution.[1] The original industrial revolution not only saw the emergence of our movement, it also marked the start of the long environmental decline that has led to the full-blown climate crisis we have today. A green industrial revolution, with unions at its heart, is what we need to reverse its impact.

Trade union members work across all sectors and industries, including the big polluting ones. As we shift away from a fossil fuel economy, we have to ensure that those workers are not left behind. My union is clear: only government investment in new sustainable technology will provide the 'just transition' from 'dirty' industries to sustainable energy and green jobs. It will retrain workers for renewable energy jobs that are high-skilled, secure and well paid, as well as delivering social justice through supporting those workers who lose their jobs as a consequence of the transition. Our movement is committed to a target of 2030 for achieving the majority of our carbon emission reductions. How long the transition takes will depend on the radicalism of the government. Leaving it to the free market will not be enough.

Toshiba's withdrawal in 2018 from a proposed nuclear plant in Moorside, scheduled to produce 7 per cent of the country's electricity, left a massive hole in the UK's plans for energy supply, decarbonisation and the economy of West Cumbria. The government's response? This is 'entirely a commercial decision for Toshiba'. The project would have provided thousands of highly skilled jobs, including for those working on the decommissioning of the Sellafield site. We can debate whether investing in nuclear power is the right way to hit targets for greenhouse gas emissions and provide energy security, and Unite firmly supports a mixed energy policy as part of the transition from fossil fuels, but Toshiba's decision was a cruel blow to the region's economy. It was a reminder that communities, jobs and livelihoods should not depend on private sector whims.

I think too of the Tories' refusal to back the Swansea Tidal Lagoon power plant. The lagoon would have been the first 'green energy' tidal power scheme in the UK. The government's rejection of it not only deprived the Welsh economy of a £500 million boost and 2,000 jobs but denied Wales the opportunity to be at the forefront of green energy innovation.

However, while energy diversification is vital to our future, we have a duty not to destroy whole communities that remain reliant on the old methods. And this takes us back to the 'just transition' debate. Unless workers, through their trade unions, are driving the transition, rather than just policymakers, then it is an effectively meaningless discussion. When working people today are more concerned about how they're going to make ends meet, we must ensure that in tackling the climate crisis we recognise the huge opportunity it gives us to reset the economy in a way that protects workers in traditional industries.

An article in the US left-wing magazine *Jacobin* reveals the understanding of a (non-union) coal miner and his fellow workers of a just transition: 'He's open to the idea of transitioning into a new job. But he needs proof that a just transition is a serious proposal. "Bring jobs in", he says. "Money talks." '[2] And: 'If these politicians who talk about climate change are against coal, they need to come to these coal places and tell people and bring jobs in.'

This is the same, relatively straightforward, argument I use in response to those who criticise me and my union over the issues of Trident and a third Heathrow runway. I am no supporter of nuclear weapons and I absolutely recognise the environmental implications of increased airport capacity, not just on the environment but on neighbouring communities. But these are good, skilled jobs, and in the absence of a government with the sort of radical vision that Labour has for alternatives, I am bound to support members whose families and communities depend on those jobs.

I have referred earlier to how badly the UK lags behind in the production of electric vehicle battery production, and how important it is to produce the robotics and batteries needed by the auto industry close to the assembly plants. If we do not do that then those plants will go elsewhere. When I visited the Nissan plant in Sunderland, where our members manufacture the all-electric Leaf model, I was impressed by the technological developments now available. As a union we must be at the forefront of campaigning to bring electric and autonomous vehicle production, along with the infrastructure, here to the UK.

This technology will reshape the automotive industry, but not in isolation. Unions are strongest when members across sectors support each other, and we must face these challenges together. The potential impact of driverless technology on workers in the auto sector is obvious, if it is left unregulated. Similarly, a decline in demand for petrol and diesel, and indeed the government's declared ban on new diesel cars by 2040, pose questions for our members on North Sea platforms, in oil refineries and behind the wheels of fuel tankers.

Trade unions must use the strength of their industrial knowledge to rise to these challenges, opportunities and threats by proposing new ideas and raising the vital questions around the development of new technologies, and by driving government to formulate an integrated industrial plan to make it happen. The biggest barrier to investment and innovation remains government inactivity. Labour is developing policies around investing in critical infrastructure and using the power of public procurement, including mandating public bodies to switch to electric vehicles. Bringing our utilities back into public ownership will also put power into the hands of working people to make the right investments. Without proper investment in research and development, public infrastructure and procurement, the UK will continue to lag behind.

If I am thinking about the opportunities for, but also the threats to the trade union movement, I must also address the rise of so-called populism and the far right in the UK and globally. Trade unionists have always stood against far-right extremism in all its guises. Whether fighting fascism in Spain with the International Brigades, occupying Cable Street to stop Mosley's Blackshirts attacking Jewish communities in the East End in 1936, standing up to the National Front in the 1970s, or opposing the numerous forms of bigotry and intolerance in society today.

Populism is not a word I enjoy. I think there's a naivety about it that disguises and mainstreams the racist policies of political parties such as UKIP and the Brexit Party. What we are seeing today is a well-financed and very sophisticated ideological attack on our fundamental values and democratic institutions, on our basic rights.

I visited an RMT picket line in Leeds with our regional committee, during the fight to keep guards on trains. The striking rail workers there had experienced first-hand the hatred the far right have for our movement. The neo-fascists had tried to intimidate them on their picket line, but we know that as long as we stand together they will never intimidate a united working class.

This is why Unite has launched our 'Unity over Division' campaign, following the unprecedented increase in far-right street activity in towns, cities and communities around the UK. Such groups have misappropriated the yellow vests of the anti-austerity protesters in Paris, which were a symbol of workers coming together in solidarity against neoliberalism. These far-right rallies, allegedly demonstrating against extremism and for free speech, are platforms for Islamophobia and racism.

After so many years of relentless austerity and cuts in services, and with right-wing political leaders who, like Trump in the US and Johnson here, think nothing of using offensive and derogatory language to describe people and their situations, we have seen a huge rise in homophobic, racial and religious attacks on our streets. Migrant workers suffer verbal abuse at work every day. In their exit interviews, migrant staff leaving the NHS have stated that a key factor was abuse from patients and constant taunts of 'go back home'. This is unacceptable in 2019.

Our trade union values are based on fairness, decency and dignity in and out of the workplace, and we have a duty as trade unionists to stand up for equality and to challenge those who attack our values. 'Unity over Division' is primarily a training and education programme aimed at equipping our officers and activists with the counter-arguments to challenge the far right's narrative, including myths around immigration, the welfare state, the NHS, education and women's rights. But as well as education, we and other unions mobilise for protests against the far right in towns and cities across the country.

It is up to us to fight for our position in a new society, socially planned and regulated by a progressive government, with powerful unions and civil society involved in charting our way forward. Reindustrialisation and automation can be steered in the right direction and their benefits reaped by society. We do not need to view the future of our economy in trepidation and fear; we can, together, fight for something better.

Trade unions underpin democracy, in a world where it is increasingly under threat. In spite of the decades of attacks aimed at undermining our influence and ability to stand up for working people, we stand defiantly uncrushed.

I only have to point to the victory of the workers in saving the iconic Harland and Wolff shipyard in Belfast. They occupied their yard, backed by their community and, with their unions standing shoulder to shoulder with them, fought for their future when others, including government ministers, had given up on them. And they won. Trade unionism at its best.

We are different groups of workers, with different histories, different militancies, or none. Trade unions have to represent all those groups in different and new ways. But always the central theme of solidarity, which we can never put a price on, shines through. Workers want to be treated fairly. That's as common as drawing breath. We fight for fairness.

Being trade unionists gives us the ability to look the boss in the eye, to look powerful people in the eye, and stand firm against injustices. And it gives us opportunities – to be educated, to become future leaders, and to meet so many good people along the way.

Unions are as necessary today as they were during and after the industrial revolution, and being an active trade unionist shows us how we can affect the lives of those around us. As trade unionists we must restore hope. To quote from Percy Bysshe Shelley's 'The Masque of Anarchy', my favourite poem, written in response to the Peterloo Massacre, we must 'rise like lions', rise to the challenges and never lose faith in our collective power.

Tony Benn told of how his father said to him: 'Dare to be a Daniel. Dare to stand alone. Dare to have a purpose firm. Dare to let it [be] known.' Now I say to my children, 'there is always more to be done. And, above all, have the courage to always be on the side of the angels.'

So that's my case: trade unionists care for people, they defend people. It's why being a trade unionist matters.

POSTSCRIPT

This book goes to print in the middle of a general election campaign. Poor timing, some might say, but it was never really intended as a political rallying cry.

I have something of a reputation for my predictions, but it's difficult to predict where we might be by the time of publication. It is said that a pessimist sees a difficulty in every opportunity while an optimist sees an opportunity in every difficulty. Well I remain optimistic, in spite of the many difficulties before us – whatever the general election produces – because we have our movement. The case for trade unionism set out here will endure, whoever is in Downing Street at the time you read this book.

Trade unions, like sport, have the power to bring people together. They are needed now, more than ever, to represent and unite people in our divided and unequal society, with or without a progressive Labour government.

Of course I have never made any secret of my support for Jeremy Corbyn or that I have waited all my life for a Labour leader dedicated to transforming our nation into one that mirrors our trade union values. During the course of writing this book, our movement has been up against the most right-wing government this country has seen for decades, a government that despises working-class people and the places we come from. It is a government awash with hedge fund cash that has the majority of the media firmly in their corner. When one fifth of our country lives on incomes below the poverty line, nearly one in three children lives in poverty and just 10 per cent of the country owns 44 per cent of the nation's wealth, never have we needed a government that serves the people as much as we do now.

But Westminster can only ever be part of the story.

As trade unionists we never cease to feel pride in who we are – the authentic voice for millions of people and for the communities of these lands. Whatever the government, the trade unions will remain the greatest force for social change that this country has, the only force able to balance the otherwise uncontrolled power of employers, which, whether they are good or bad, will always ultimately be driven by the principle of profit maximisation. Trade unionism is the bulwark of democracy, of proper welfare provision, of gender and racial equality and of anti-fascism and peace. Everything in fact that marks civilisation out from barbarism.

While I don't dispute for a moment the part played by others in many of our progressive achievements, history tells us that only an organised working class has achieved the strength to impose our values on the powerful.

Finally, I am well aware that there will be those who criticise me for not devoting space to the tumultuous events since 2016's European Union referendum and the more than three years of shambolic Tory Brexit negotiations and parliamentary deadlock that have followed.

One thing I can be certain about is that the UK will not have left the EU by the time this book is published. I'm often accused of being pro-Brexit, yet I also hear calls for me to step in and stop Brexit. The first is untrue and the second a feat well beyond my powers. To be clear, Unite campaigned harder than any trade union for Remain. It is an inconvenient truth for some people that we lost, but it must be recognised. Labour adopted a 2017 manifesto, which so many Remainers embraced, that pledged to negotiate a Brexit deal that puts our economy and living standards first. That is why Labour and the trade unions worked so hard to fend off the horrors of a no-deal Brexit.

I have always supported Labour's approach to bringing our country together by trying to speak to all of it, not just half of it while dismissing the other half, as the other main parties have done. But even as I write about Leave and Remain, I reject these labels. In or out of the EU, it is the class questions that matter. Whether we are 'leavers' or 'remainers' matters far less than our class, our socialism and our internationalism. As trade unionists we are united under one banner, and with that unity comes the responsibility to advance our values of solidarity, community, equality and social justice.

As trade unionists we can only express those values by being at the forefront of the political, industrial and community resistance to austerity and to right-wing governments everywhere. When working people stand together, anything is possible. And that is the case for trade unions.

NOTES

1 Hope in My Heart

1 BBC Radio 4, *Political Thinking with Nick Robinson*, 'The Len McCluskey One', at bbc.co.uk.
2 Jack Jones, 'A World to Win', Birkbeck College, 1975 (Foundation Oration).

2 Giving a Voice

1 See 'The Struggle for Democracy: Trade Unionism', National Archives, at nationalarchives.gov.uk.
2 The Union Makes Us Strong, 'The Match Workers Strike Fund Register', at unionhistory.info.
3 TUC, 'The Great 1889 Dockers' Strike', at tuc.org.uk.
4 Encyclopaedia Britannica, 'Taff Vale case (1900–1901)', at britannica. com.
5 Terry McCarthy, '*A Short History of the British Labour Movement, from a Socialist Perspective*', Labour History Movement Publications, 2017.
6 Eileen Turnbull and Carolyn Jones, 'One Step Forward for

Shrewsbury Pickets', *Morning Star*, 13 December 2018.

7 Dan Milmo, 'British Airways Settles Cabin Crew Dispute', *Guardian*, 22 June 2011.

8 Unite the Union, 'Fair Tips for Waiting Staff', 7 June 2019, at unitetheunion.org.

9 'Fringe Venue Pledges Fair Conditions for All Following "Landmark" Agreement', *Edinburgh News*, 27 July 2018.

3 Unity Is Strength

1 TUC, 'Join a Union', at tuc.org.uk.

2 'Google Workers Stage Global Walkout Over Treatment of Female Workers', *I News*, 1 November 2018, at inews.co.uk.

3 'Drivers Walk Out for Second Day', *Oxford Mail*, 6 March 2017.

4 Unite, 'Bad Bosses Be Warned', 2 July 2018, at unitetheunion.org.

5 Brian Reade, 'Dockers Sacked for Refusing to Cross Picket Line Create Hub to Help Workers in Need', *Daily Mirror*, 4 September 2018.

6 Robert Colville, 'The True Scandal of Lifting the Public Sector Pay Cap is the Left's Whining', *Sun*, 27 July 2018.

4 A World without Unions

1 'Employment Tribunal Fees May be Resurrected, MoJ Confirms', *Law Society Gazette*, 7 November 2018.

2 Tim Lezard, 'Unite Wins Landmark Holiday Pay Legal Case', 1 August 2017, at union-news.co.uk.

3 Dave Smith 'The forgotten spycops inquiry and why it's so important for the Labour Party', *Morning Star*, 25 September 2018.

4 Kevin McKenna, 'Remember When the Unions Could Take on a Dictator? These Three Do . . .', *Guardian*, 11 November 2018.

5 Mattha Busby, 'Labour: We'll Restore Right to Strike in Support of Overseas Workers', *Guardian*, 8 December 2018.

6 ILO, 'C087 – Freedom of Association and Protection of the Right to Organise Convention, 1948 (No. 87)', and 'C098 – Right to Organise and Collective Bargaining Convention, 1949 (No. 98)', both at ilo.org.

7 *Middlebrook Mushrooms Ltd v Transport and General Workers' Union* [1993] IRLR 232, CA, at app.croneri.co.uk.

8 Haroon Siddique, 'Uber Eats Couriers' Pay Protest Brings Traffic to a Halt in Central London', *Guardian*, 20 September 2018.

9 Margaret Thatcher, 'Remarks Visiting Finchley', 14 July 1984, at margaretthatcher.org.

10 Will Hutton, Patrick Wintour and Andrew Adonis, 'Blair in 1997 "I am going to be a lot more radical in government than people think" ', *Guardian*, 27 April 1997.

11 Office for National Statistics, 'Productivity Measures', at ons.gov.uk.

12 'Surge in Low-value Jobs Magnifies UK Productivity Problem', *Financial Times*, 12 August 2018.

13 Department for Business, Energy and Industrial Strategy, 'Building our Industrial Strategy', Green Paper, January 2017, at beisgovuk. citizenspace.com.

14 Ian McConnell, 'Workers at Alexander Dennis are Entitled to Share in the Success', *The Herald*, 27 September 2013.

15 'British Bank RBS Hires "Digital Human" Cora on Probation', *Reuters*, 21 February 2018.

16 World Economic Forum, 'Five Million Jobs by 2020: The Real Challenge of the Fourth Industrial Revolution', 18 January 2016, at weforum.org.

17 Unite, 'Industrial Strategy: Building an Economy That Works for All – Unite's Submission to the BEIS Industrial Strategy Green Paper', April 2017.

18 Jasper Jolley, 'UK Car Industry Future Hinges "not on Brexit, but on batteries" ', *Guardian*, 7 July 2019.

19 'Desperate Amazon Workers "forced to sleep in tents so they can be at work on time" ', *Metro*, 19 December 2016.

20 Robert Booth, 'DPD Courier Who Was Fined For Day Off to See Doctor Dies from Diabetes', *Guardian*, 5 February 2018.

5 We Are Family

1 A Web of English History, 'Trade Unions 1830–1851', at history-home.co.uk.

2 Peter Walker, 'Divided Britain: Study Finds Huge Chasm in Attitudes', *Guardian*, 17 October 2017.

3 Labour Party, 'Alternative Models of Ownership: Report to the Shadow Chancellor of the Exchequer and Shadow Secretary of State for Business, Energy and Industrial Strategy', at labour.org.uk.

4 Larry Elliot, 'Theresa May Misses a Trick After U-Turn Over Workers on Boards', *Guardian*, 10 June 2018.

5 Mariana Mazzucato, *The Value of Everything*, Penguin, 2019.

6 See www.thepeoplesassembly.org.uk.

7 Mark Lyon, *The Battle of Grangemouth: A Worker's Story*, Lawrence and Wishart, 2017.

8 Emma Munbodh, 'Amazon UK Staff to Stage Protest Against "Robot" Working Conditions on Black Friday', *Daily Mirror*, 22 November 2018.

6 Playing Our Part in Politics

1 Andrew Murray and Lindsey German, *Stop the War*, Bookmarks Publications, 2005.

2 BEIS, 'Trade Union Political Funds: A Guide for Trade Unions, Their Members and Others', February 2018, at assets.publishing.service.gov.uk.

3 Andrew Murray, *A New Labour Nightmare: The Return of the Awkward Squad*, Verso, 2003.

4 Alex Nunns, *The Candidate*, Or Books, 2018 (2nd edition).

5 Jennie Formby, 'We Are Grabbing This Opportunity with Both Hands', *Labour List*, 1 March 2014, at labourlist.org.

6 Unite, 'Unite in Politics Future Candidate Programme', at unite-theunion.org.

7 Fighting for Equality

1 Ben Chu, 'Fat Cat Friday: FTSE 100 Executives Earn 133 Times More Than Average UK Worker', *Independent*, 4 January 2019.

2 *Pickstone v Freemans plc* [1989] AC 66 House of Lords, at e-

lawresources.co.uk.

3 Patricia Wynn Davies, 'Landmark Victory for Women in Fight for
   Equal Pay', *Independent*, 4 April 1997.

4 Warwick University Modern Records Centre, ' "Rouse, Ye Women":
   The Cradley Heath Chain Makers' Strike, 1910', at warwick.ac.uk.

5 Dominic Cavendish, 'Made in Dagenham, Adelphi Theatre, Review:
   Larger Than Life', *Telegraph*, 6 November 2014.

6 Striking Women, 'The Grunwick Dispute', at striking-women.org.

7 'Two Strikes and You're Out at LSG Sky Chefs', *The Caterer*, 3
   December 1998, at thecaterer.com.

8 Striking Women, 'The Gate Gourmet Dispute', at striking-women.
   org.

9 'Union Apology After 1960s Bristol Buses Race Row', BBC News, 26
   February 2013, at bbc.co.uk.

10 Unite Education, 'Mohammad Taj: Steering from the Front', 2018, at
   markwritecouk.files.wordpress.com.

8 Conclusion: Rise Like Lions

1 Rebecca Long-Bailey, 'Why Labour Is Calling for a Green Jobs
   Revolution', *Labour List*, 23 November 2018, at labourlist.org.

2 ' "They're Not Moving until We Get Paid": An Interview with Josh
   Holbrook', *Jacobin*, 6 August 2019, at jacobinmag.com.